The Easy 5-Ingredients Or Less Instant Pot Cookbook

101 Quick, Simple And Delicious Recipes Made For Your Instant Pot High Pressure Cooker Cooking At Home

By Jessica C. Waston

Contents

Introduction

Hello friend, this is Olivia Fisher! Firstly thank and congratulate you for purchasing this book: "*The Easy 5-Ingredients Or Less Instant Pot Cookbook-101 Quick, Simple And Delicious Recipes Made For Your Instant Pot High Pressure Cooker Cooking At Home*". Hope this book will be your good choice on amazon!

Do you have an Instant Pot or wanna have one?
Do you want to have easy and delicious foods made just in 5 ingredients or less?
Do you want to be professional about using instant pot pressure cooker?

When it comes to cooking there are all sorts of modern time-saving devices. One of those is the Instant Pot. The Instant Pot is a seven-in-one kitchen appliance, which combines seven different time-saving devices into one solid kitchen unit. As such it makes life and cooking incredibly practical and easy to create all your favourite dishes in various settings in mere minutes.

In this book you will discover the multiple functions of an instant pot, how it is different to a pressure cooker or a slow cooker, how you can make delicious, simple recipes in it and less than $1/10^{th}$ of the time a normal recipe would take!

No need to be an expert chef. No need to have all evening to yourself. You don't even need much money! These delicious and simple recipes are easy for anyone to pull off, and you will not miss your old fast food and microwave lifestyle. So whether you are a busy family, a working professional, or a student, the instant pot will be your kitchen friend for many years to come.

Inside this book, you will find a large amount of delicious recipes, including: **Meat Dishes, Poultry Dishes, Vegetarian Dishes, Soup, Side Dishes & Desserts**. Each will be marked if the recipe is 'Dairy Free (not including eggs)' (DF), 'Gluten Free' (GF),or 'Vegan' (V). We have also included a key for 'Low carb' (LC) and 'Low Fat' (LF).

All recipes can be made with 5 ingredients or less (okay there are one or two where an extra sixth ingredient was absolutely necessary, but we know you'll forgive us once you taste them!) , apart from the addition of oil in the bottom of the Instant Pot, where advised, and salt and pepper for basic seasoning and flavour. All the recipes are well-chosen and chef proved. You will find your favorite ones!

This book will lead you from a newer to professional about instant pot using! This book will provide you 101 easy and delicious recipes which all are made in just 5 ingredients or less to save you time and money! This book will be your lifelong companion for your cooking! Now all you need to do is read it and put it into action!

Chapter 1: What is an Instant Pot?

By now I am sure you have the raving and great reviews of instant pots. After all, you're here, looking for recipes!

An instant pot allows you to make use of several different cooking functions in one handy appliance. The idea is that it will save you time, electricity, and counter space, at the same time allowing you to eat healthier every day.

A brief history

The instant pot was first imagined in 2009 by The Instant Pot Company in Canada. The creators had experience in technical background and food preparation, and wanted to find a solution that would allow busy people to move away from fast food and snacks onto a healthier diet. The only way to do this is to allow people to make healthy food, in their own home, in the same amount of time it would take them to place an order online, or go to the shops or a restaurant. No simple challenge!

In 2010 the first model was released. It allowed you to cook five different ways in the same machine, by using an advanced microprocessor. Buyers were thrilled at the prospect of being able to cook everything in one single pot.

This provided the motivation for The Instant Pot Company to make the model we are using, with seven different functions. Most recently, in 2014, they also released a ten in one Bluetooth enabled instant pot; allowing you to monitor and adapt your cooking from a mobile app. Whatever will they think of next?

How does it work?

The instant pot has seven different functions combined into one. But how did they do this?

The first step is making the instant pot programmable. The instant pot uses state of the art micro-processing to turn subtle nuances of heat, pressure, and time, into press-of-the-button affairs. Much like hitting "enter" on your computer could send a message, open a document, start a paragraph, or play a movie depending on what program you are using, with the instant pot, hitting enter you can adjust times and plans will have a different effect depending on which instant pot function you are using.

The main function of an instant pot is pressure cooking. Pressure cooking involves combining heat and intense pressure to help food break down, speeding up the cooking process massively. The pressure is controlled by a valve which can be used to build or release pressure manually if needs be.

However they have also incorporated the other great kitchen gadget, the slow cooker, into the instant pot's functions. Slow cooking involves applying slight heat for a longer period of time to cook food through, meaning you can put all your ingredients in the pot in the morning and have a stew by lunch or dinner.

It only took some tweaking to turn the slow cooking function into a perfect rice cooker. A rice cooker gently heats water around rice, encouraging it to absorb the hot water and cook perfectly. This is better than cooking rice in a pot as it prevents sticking and water excess, resulting in a fresh load of perfectly cooked fluffy rice every time.

For the truly healthy experience, you can steam in your instant pot. Your instant pot includes a Steam basket. Simply place your food in the Steam basket, add water to the body of the pot, and set to Steam for freshly steamed food. You can even cook bread and cakes using this trick!

You can also braise and fry in your instant pot. Keeping the lid open you can set the temperature nice and high, add some oil, and simply cook your food in the base of the open pot, just like you would with an ordinary frying pan. This trick lets you prepare meats and vegetables for a stew, or cook down onions before beginning to assemble a larger dish.

Yoghurt fans will be pleased to find out they can make their own yoghurt in an instant pot. The Yoghurt setting takes a process which normally involves hours of work and many different pots and bowls, and makes it fast, easy, and one-pot only!

Finally, a function all of us can appreciate, the instant pot can safely warm your food. Food needs to be warmed quickly, and to a certain temperature, otherwise the warmth can encourage bacteria to breed. Like the top setting on a microwave, the instant pot's Warm setting heats food up just right, although it is still not recommended to leave food warming too long!

The features and functions of an Instant Pot.

What flexibility does this variety of functions offer? Almost limitless flexibility!

Because of all the different functions, you can do almost anything except deep fry or roast in your instant pot. Unless you need to cook two things at the same time, you can theoretically complete your whole cooking process in just this one device.

For example you can make rice, then stir and fry the rice, then seal it and steam some meat on top before serving. Or you can brown some onions and vegetables, deglaze, and stew them.

What is more, the instant pot makes all this incredibly safe! Besides the seven settings, your instant pot comes equipped to handle intense pressure with a solid lid, guide lines to show you how much to fill it, and a manual release valve to let the pressure out when you need to.

It also has eight pre-set settings with times already assigned to them, so if you know just what you are cooking you can just hit a button and it will decide the temperature, pressure, and time all for you!

If you want to use a pre-set setting for a different amount of time, just hit the plus or minus button to adjust the time up or down until it is right for your recipe.

Your instant pot will make pressure cooking, slow cooking, and all other sorts of cooking really quick, and super simple!

What are all these buttons and what do they do?

An instant pot may be a bit intimidating at first. However you will see that every button is neatly labelled, and their functions are actually pretty intuitive.

Soup: High pressure cook for 30 minutes., great for extracting juices without drying.

Meat/Stew: High pressure cook for 35 minutes., perfect for tenderizing meat and breaking down starches and proteins.

Bean/Chili: A high pressure cook for 30 minutes. for hydrating and cooking legumes.

Poultry: High pressure 15 minute cook time making sure poultry is cooked thoroughly and safe to eat but not dry.

Rice: A low pressure fully automatic program that will cook rice and milled oats.

Multi-grain: High pressure 40 minute cook time, ideal for all whole grains.

Porridge: High pressure 20 minute cook time for whole oat porridge.

Steam: High pressure 10 minute cook time, perfect for heating water just high enough to provide steam to cook things in.

Some new models have the added Cake, Egg, and Sterilize functions, designed to make moist cakes, boil eggs soft or hard, and sterilize items, and vegetables.

Chapter 2: Why use an Instant Pot?

But why should we bother with an instant pot? After all, it's a bit of an investment, and can't we just do all these things anyway, but in our own homes, with the kitchen equipment we already have? Well, there are actually four great reasons why an instant pot is a better investment than any other kitchen gadget.

1: Quick cooking.

With an instant pot you will slash your cooking time right down. The high pressure of the pressure cooking option lets you cook food in sometimes as little as a tenth of the time it would take to cook normally. This is especially true of things that take a while to cook, like dried beans. A pressure cooker can also minimize or even prevent sticking, which is great for starchy foods and foods prone to burning.

With the slow cooking mode you can still cut down your cooking time. Simply drop all your ingredients in your instant pot, set to slow cook, and let it simmer down for 4-10 hours. You will get all the goodness of a home-prepared stew with almost no effort at all.

Because you use so few pots and pans, there is much less clean up time, making your cooking more efficient. Simply clean out the insert and lid of your instant pot, as well as any bowls you used for mixing. Many dishes can even be mixed in your instant pot, and the frying or reducing stages of making things can be done in the instant pot too, really saving dish washing time.

2: Compact cooking.

With an instant pot not only can you get rid of your pots and pans, you can enjoy all the functions of a pressure cooker, slow cooker, rice cooker, Steam, etc, in one handy pot. Your instant pot will only take up as much space as a slow cooker, or a rice cooker, but does virtually everything you need, saving you valuable counter, shelf, and cupboard space.

Because it heats so quickly and has a warm setting, you can even use it to replace your microwave! Simply keep your leftovers in heat-proof bowls and when it's time to reheat them either empty the food into your instant pot and warm it, or put the bowl in your Steam basket and use the Steam setting to heat and/or cook through!

You can use this if you have a smaller kitchen, if you need your counter for anything, or if you are using your stove top. In smaller kitchens an instant pot can replace a lot of bulky kitchen equipment, giving you more space for the most important things. If you have a cluttered counter your kitchen can feel cramped and be hard to work in, so using an instant pot can help you by eliminating the need for multiple gadgets. And if you are cooking up a huge feast and your whole stovetop and oven are busy, you can use your instant pot as an extra cooking device. Genius!

3: Safe cooking.

Because your instant pot has high walls and can cook fully sealed, you will eliminate the risks associated with standard pots and pans. A normal pot or pan puts you at risk of splattering oil or bubbling water, which could burn you. It also involves a hot flame or ring. Your instant pot takes away most of the dangerous elements of cooking, making it much safer.

As it can be used with metals, it is a great replacement for a microwave. Microwaves cannot reheat things in metal containers, or with metal cutlery in them. But your instant pot can handle metal safely.

As it is a very modern pressure cooker, you are reducing the risk associated with the stovetop pressure cooker. Stovetop pressure cookers do not always lock well, and you need to monitor the temperature and pressure gauges to make sure that everything is going well. Your instant pot self-regulates in terms of temperature and pressure, making it a safe pressure cooking option.

Although you should never leave it on when you are out of the house, you can leave it cooking as you go about your business at home. Simply set it to slow cook and catch up on TV, do the housework, or work from home. When you are done you will have a delicious meal from almost no effort!

4: Economical in the long run.

There are many foods which are cheaper because they take longer to cook. This is the law of supply and demand: because most people do not have the time and tools to cook these foods, most people will not buy them, so they sell them cheap to get rid of them. But most of these foods are super healthy for us and full of flavor. And we can get the benefit of these foods so easily using our instant pot!

Imagine the money you could save by using tough cuts of meat. Beef cuts like the diaphragm, rump, stewing steak, and heart are not usually enjoyed because you need to break down all the cartilage in them to make them juicy and tender. But with your instant pot you can get them cooked right down in no time!

You can also save money using dried legumes. Dried legumes are so much cheaper than canned, and better for the planet, and are not salted so they are better for your health. Again, normally you need to soak and stew them for ages to make it worthwhile, but with an instant pot you slow cook them in less time until they are tender.

Your instant pot cooks so fast, buying broths and sauces will be a thing of the past. A tomato sauce, BBQ sauce, or cheese sauce is only minute away, for a fraction of the cost of buying it bottled.

And if you need a quick meal, your instant pot can bring you a healthy meal as quickly as you can heat a ready-made-meal or order take out! Just find a 10-20 minute recipe, add the ingredients, and enjoy your quick, healthy meal.

So eventually your instant pot will more than pay for itself. You have everything to gain and nothing to lose!

Chapter 3: Instant Pot Tips, Tricks, Do's and Don'ts.

Like with all cooking appliances, there is a right way and a wrong way to use your instant pot. By keeping an eye on what you are doing you can make sure that your instant pot is safe, quick to use, and lasts a very long time. If you do not follow these simple guidelines you risk wasting your time, breaking your instant pot, and even hurting yourself.

DO'S

DO: Watch out about overfilling. Your instant pot should not be completely filled. Ever! You need space for pressure and/or steam to build up. Whether you are filling it with food or fluid, always make sure there is plenty of space from the top.

DO: Experiment with the functions. Your instant pot does so many things, don't just use it for pressure cooking and get other pots and gadgets for the rest. Otherwise what's the point in having it? Use it to shallow fry, boil, steam, bake, etc. The possibilities are plentiful.

DO: Use more dry legumes. Dry legumes are a great protein source, cheap, and absorb flavors so well. Now, that you can cook them in a heartbeat, make sure to use them whenever you can.

DO: Measure your liquids carefully. Your instant pot has two different limits: the pressure limit and the slow cooker limit. Do not exceed the fluid amount for either! Always count things that liquefy, like gelatine or sugar, as a liquid.

DO: Be careful handling steam. Steam and pressure are nothing to joke around with! Never put your hand right in the steam, and always release the pressure according to the instructions manual. Always seal your instant pot properly before building pressure. Always open it when it is ready.

DO: Clean it well after each use. Your instant pot will not last if it ends up with a built up film of fat or layer of burnt and sticky food in it. Besides, that is unhealthy. Even if you have "only" used it to steam, remember that steam carries fat particles and creates a greasy film, so it still needs cleaning.

DON'TS

DON'T: Give up at the first hurdle. Sometimes with new kitchen gadgets we find them a little awkward at first. But the instant pot is super intuitive, so even if you have a couple of setbacks, you'll figure it out in under a week.

DON'T: Put things in in huge pieces. Even cooking is important, and big pieces do not respond as well to pressure or quick cooking. Leave the whole chickens for slow cooking only.

DON'T: Put it on the stove top. This is not a traditional pressure cooker! Putting it in direct contact with any heat source except its own heating element is dangerous and should **never** be done.

DON'T: Miss any pieces when cooking. Another dangerous thing! Make sure you always put the insert in, or you could cause an electrical short. And don't forget to use your different pieces properly, such as steam basket, or you could ruin your food.

DON'T: Use quick release unless specified. The pressure that can build up in your instant pot is intense. If you release it too fast you could get hurt. Only use quick release when a recipe specifically calls for it.

DON'T: Use it when you are not home. Unlike with a traditional slow cooker, the instant pot reaches high temperatures, can carry a high voltage, and involves literal pressure. Do not leave the house when it is on.

DON'T: Fill it with hot oil. This is not a deep fat fryer! Filling it with oil is dangerous and could cause a grease fire. At the very least, you will break your instant pot.

DON'T: Try and force it open. Again: intense pressure. Forcing it open could cause a seriously painful blast.

Chapter 4: Instant Pot Recipes

Getting on to the 'meat' of the book, we can finally begin to check out some recipes! Before we get to the recipes themselves, it is important that you read the recipes carefully and bear in mind that if you are using another brand of multi-cooker or a different model of instant pot you may need to adjust what you are doing to account for that.

Why 5 Ingredients or Less?

We all lead busy lives and because of this we seem to have less time to devote to cooking. The more ingredients a recipe has, the harder it is to fit into our busy lives. We need to make sure we have all the ingredients we need, balance flavors, prepare all the ingredients, and make sure they get the right cooking time.

By keeping the ingredients list simple, we maximize health and flavor but minimize the amount of time it takes to prepare the meal.

Notes about these recipes

Added to these recipes are dietary guidelines. These ensure you know when a recipe will be suitable for your personal diet. Each will be marked if the recipe is 'Dairy Free (not including eggs)' (DF), 'Gluten Free' (GF),or 'Vegan' (V). We have also included a key for 'Low carb' (LC) and 'Low Fat' (LF).

Notes on timing

The timing calculated here is a rough expectation. It could take a little more or a little less depending on the size of your cuts and the size of your instant pot. If you are in doubt, cut the time down a little and see how your cooking goes.

Like with any piece of cooking equipment, you need to get a proper feel for your instant pot. Work out what works best for different types of foods, different days, different pressure levels. Look out for warning signs when things go wrong. Develop a relationship with your instant pot. It will be your best friend in the kitchen!

Notes on Ingredients

There are only five ingredients or less per recipe(okay there are one or two where an extra sixth ingredient was absolutely necessary, but we know you'll forgive us once you taste them!) , apart from the addition of oil in the bottom of the Instant Pot, where advised, and salt and pepper for basic seasoning and flavour. Water needed may not be included in that five, especially for steam. This limited number of ingredients does not mean you cannot switch them around for an equal volume, or add things. Just always make sure that when you add something new, you take away some of the rest! You don't want to risk overfilling your instant pot. And always remember that some solids count as liquids because they liquefy when heated, such as jellies, jams, sugars, and fats!

When it comes to special diets, look for substitutes that are about the same in texture, or that have a similar cooking time. The flavor will be different, but sometimes a substitute with a similar flavor has a very different cooking time, which could add to the work you are doing.

Notes on Measurements

All measurements are in US standard; cups, teaspoons, tablespoons, ounces, and pounds. There are simple conversion charts available online for people who use different units of measurement. However, always remember that the measurements for a recipe are only a guideline. You may prefer more of something or less of something. And if you have roughly as much as you need, being off by a little bit here or there will not hurt your meal.

Even though with the recipe you can mix and match a bit, ALWAYS follow your instant pot's instructions to the letter. If the amount in your recipe would overfill your instant pot, cut it down a little. If you look in and see there is not enough fluid, add some. It will not hurt your recipe to add a tablespoon less potato or a quarter of a cup more water, but it can break your instant pot if you overfill it or underwater it.

Meat Dishes

1. African Beef & Peanut Stew(DF, GF, LC)

Categories: DF, GF, LC
Serves: 6
Preparation time: 60 minutes
Ingredients:
32 oz stewing beef
4 teaspoons red curry powder
3 inches fresh ginger
2 onions
¾ cup creamy peanut butter

Preparation:
1) Dice up the beef, and toss the meat chunks through the curry powder.
2) Set the Instant Pot to Saute, and brown the beef. It may need to be done in 2 batches. Cook each batch for 3-4 minutes and turn often so that it's all evenly browned.
3) Peel and slice the onions, and add them into the pot with the second batch of meat.
4) Then, add in 3 cups of water and season well with salt and pepper.
5) Stir in the peanut butter, and grate in the ginger.
6) Set the pot to a Stew, or Meat setting, if yours has one, and cook on High Pressure for 35 minutes. Then, allow a natural release and enjoy!

Serving Suggestion: Chop some roasted peanuts and have them on top as a garnish.

Tip: To bulk this out, you can add in hearty veggies such as pumpkin, squash or carrots.

2. Balsamic Beef(DF, GF, LC)

Categories: DF, GF, LC
Serves: 4-6
Preparation time: 60 minutes
Ingredients:
48 oz chuck beef roasting joint
3 garlic cloves
1 sprig fresh rosemary
1 sprig fresh thyme
¼ cup balsamic vinegar

Preparation:

1) Slice the garlic thinly.
2) Slice little holes into the beef, and put the garlic slices into the holes.
3) Take the leaves from the thyme and rosemary, and mix them together with some salt and pepper. Then, rub this mix all over the meat.
4) Set the Instant Pot to Saute and heat 1 tablespoon of oil in there. When it's warm, add in the beef joint and brown on all sides.
5) Pour in 1 cup of water along with the balsamic vinegar, and scrape any bits from around the edges into the mixture.
6) Cook on High Pressure for 40 minutes, and then allow a Natural Release.
7) Shred the beef a little and enjoy with some of the cooking juices.

Serving Suggestion: Try this with our Cajun Greens recipe – it's a delicious, low carb combination!

Tip: Really make sure that the meat is nicely browned all over before steaming to get that nice extra flavour and slight crunchiness to your beef.

3. BBQ Beef Meatballs(DF, LC)

Categories: DF, LC
Serves: 4
Preparation time: 20 minutes
Ingredients:
48 oz frozen beef meatballs
18 oz grape jelly
18 oz BBQ sauce

Preparation:

1) Pour 1 cup of water into the bottom of your Instant Pot, and place the steaming basket inside.
2) Put the meatballs onto the steaming rack and cook for 5 minutes on High Pressure, and then quick release it.
3) Remove the meatballs from the pot, and pour out the water. Add in the grape jelly and BBQ sauce and set the pot onto Saute.
4) Stir until the sauce is smooth and beginning to bubble, and then stir the meatballs through again.

Serving Suggestion: If you don't eat these in one sitting, they are great to refrigerate and have in a salad the next day too.

Tip: Taste the sauce and add in extra seasonings or flavours to your liking.

4. Beer BBQ Ribs(DF, LC)

Categories: DF, LC
Serves: 4
Preparation time: 60 minutes
Ingredients:
48 oz beef baby back ribs
12 oz bbq sauce
1 cup beer
1 onion
1 teaspoon paprika

Preparation:

1) Cut the ribs into individual servings.
2) Rub the paprika over the ribs.
3) Add a little water into the bottom of your Instant Pot and set it to sauté. Quickly brown the ribs on all over.
4) Chop the onion and add to the pot.
5) Remove the onion and ribs, and insert a rack into the pot.
6) Pour the beer into the bottom, and load the ribs and onion on top of the rack.
7) Set on High Pressure and cook for 35 minutes, and then naturally release the pressure.
8) Remove the rack from the cooker, and stir the barbecue sauce into the liquid at the bottom. Place the ribs into the sauce and simmer for 10-15 minutes to reduce the sauce down.

Serving Suggestion: Make roasted vegetable chips and a huge salad to go with these delicious ribs.

Tip: For a thicker sauce, remove some of the liquid from the bottom before adding the barbecue sauce.

5. Beef & Onion Brisket(DF, GF LC)

Categories: DF, GF LC
Serves: 6
Preparation time: At least 6 hours
Ingredients:
54 oz beef brisket
24 oz onions
6 garlic cloves
2 cups beef broth
2 tablespoons Worcestershire sauce

Preparation:

1) Set the Instant Pot to Saute and peel and quarter the onions before adding them in. Add a little oil, and let them start cooking down for 20 minutes.
2) Pat the brisket beef dry and rub in salt and pepper.
3) Remove the onions and add the brisket into the pot on Saute.
4) Mince the garlic and add it into the pot.
5) Sear the brisket for 3-5 minutes on each side. Then, add the onions back into the pot.
6) Pour in the beef broth and the Worcestershire sauce.
7) Set the pot to Low Pressure for 6-8 hours, and allow the pressure to release naturally.
8) Let the brisket sit for 25 minutes before slicing. Enjoy!

Serving Suggestion: Home-made coleslaw is a great side to keep this low carb.

Tip: Add in other vegetables to slow cook along with the beef if you like!

6. Curry Goat(DF, GF, LC, LF)

Categories: DF, GF, LC, LF
Serves: 4
Preparation time: 20 minutes
Ingredients:
17 ½ oz frozen, diced goat shoulder
8 garlic cloves
3 tablespoons curry powder (or a mix of curry powder and chilli powder)
1 tablespoon ginger
½ cup tomato paste

Preparation:

1) Set the Instant Pot to Sauté and add a little oil in to lightly coat the bottom of the pot. Once it's heated, add in the goat shoulder.
2) Season with salt and pepper and then stir the goat occasionally for 5 minutes to brown. Remove the goat and cooking juice and set aside.
3) Mince the garlic and the ginger and add them into the pot. Add a tiny bit of extra oil if necessary.
4) Then, stir in your chilli powder and allow the mixture to mix and become fragrant for about 2 minutes.
5) Pour in ¼ cup of water to scrape ay bits off of the sides, and then add another cup of water.
6) Add the goat and its juices back into the pot and cook at High Pressure for 40 minutes, and then allow a Natural Release.

Serving Suggestion: This is a great meal to make ahead, if you're having dinner for just 1 or 2, and then refrigerate overnight and have for lunch the next day. The great thing about curry is that the flavours mature and it just gets better!

Tip: If you want to thicken your sauce, stir in 2 tablespoons of almond flour.

7. Hawaiian Meatballs(DF, LF)

Categories: DF, LF
Serves: 4
Preparation time: 40 minutes
Ingredients:
14 oz pineapple chunks with juice
1 red pepper
1 pack low fat meatballs
1 tablespoon soy sauce
¾ cup brown sugar

Preparation:

1) Put the Instant Pot to Saute and add in the pineapple, meatballs, soy sauce and sugar.
2) Slice and de-seed the peppers and add them into the pot too.
3) After 3 minutes, and set to High Pressure for 5 minutes. Quick release the pressure and enjoy!

Serving Suggestion: Sticky rice!!

Tip: If you want a thicker sauce, you can stir in a tablespoon of corn starch after you're released the pressure.

8. Hot Dogs(DF, LC)

Categories: DF, LC
Serves: 3
Preparation time: 20 minutes
Ingredients:
6 hot dogs
1 tablespoon red wine vinegar
½ teaspoon cumin

Preparation:

1) Into the Instant Pot, pour the red wine vinegar and 4 cups of water.
2) Stir in the cumin and add in the hot dogs.
3) Cook on Low Pressure for 3 minutes and then allow natural release.

Serving Suggestion: Serve with salad and sides for a low carb meal. If low carb isn't on the list for you, then of course, hot dog buns and corn on the cob it is!

Tip: Spice up the water with chilli powder too, if you like it spicy.

9. Kalua Pork(DF, GF, LC)

Categories: DF, GF, LC
Serves: 4
Preparation time: 115 minutes
Ingredients:
6 garlic cloves
3 slices of bacon
1 ½ tablespoons Hawaiian rock salt
1 pork shoulder
1 cabbage

Preparation:
1) Set the Instant Pot to Saute and add the bacon into the bottom of the pan.
2) Chop the pork into 3 roughly equal-sized pieces. Cut 2 slits into each piece and tuck a garlic clove into each slit.
3) Rub the salt all over the pork.
4) Place the pork on top of the bacon, not overlapping the pork pieces, if there's room. Add in 1 cup of water.
5) Set to High Pressure for 90 minutes, and allow the pressure to release naturally. Check that the pork is tender enough to fall apart. If not, pressure cook for another 5-10 minutes. Then, remove the pork from the pot.
6) Core and chop the cabbage into wedges, and add it into the pot with the cooking liquid. Cook on High Pressure for 5 minutes.
7) Meanwhile, use 2 forks to shred the pork.
8) Pile the cooked cabbage on top of the pork and serve, using the cooking juices if needed.

Serving Suggestion: Straight into white rolls with barbecue sauce, corn on the cob and salad, am I right?

Tip: You can put the pork in to cook in the morning and leave! The pressure can naturally release itself and you'll have perfect pork to come home to.

10. Korean Beef(DF, LC, LF)

Categories: DF, LC, LF
Serves: 6
Preparation time: 70 minutes
Ingredients:
64 oz stewing beef
5 garlic cloves
1 green apple
1 tablespoon fresh ginger
½ cup soy sauce

Preparation:

1) If not done already, chop the beef into 1 inch cubes. Then, season well with salt and pepper.
2) Set the Instant Pot to Saute and add in the beef to begin browning it. Make sure to turn it to get an even cook all around.
3) Once the meat is all browned, pour in 1 cup of water and scrape down the edges. Then, add in the soy sauce.
4) Mince the garlic and ginger and stir it into the stew.
5) Peel and dice the apple, and put it into the pot, on top of the meat.
6) Cook on High Pressure for 45 minutes, and then naturally release the steam.
7) If you like, shred the meat a little more with a fork before serving.

Serving Suggestion: To keep this low fat and low carb, serve cold and mixed through an interesting salad.

Tip: As always, add chilli if needed!

11. Pork Lettuce Wraps(DF, GF, LC, LF)

Categories: DF, GF, LC, LF
Serves: 4
Preparation time: 15 minutes
Ingredients:
16 oz ground pork
8 green onions
2 heads Boston lettuce
¼ cup fresh cilantro
¼ cup lime juice

Preparation:

1) Set the Instant Pot to Saute and add in a tablespoon of oil. Add in the pork to begin to brown.
2) After 5 minutes or so, the pork should be cooked through and crumbly. Then, chop the green onions and stir them through. Also, mince the cilantro and stir in through. Then, stir in the lime juice and season well with salt and pepper.
3) Wash through the lettuce leaves and separate them.
4) Spoon around 2 tablespoons of mixture into each lettuce leaf and enjoy! Hold the wraps together with a toothpick if you like.

Serving Suggestion: A super fresh salad of carrot, cucumber and radish, with a complementary lime and olive oil dressing will make this dish!

Tip: You can add a pulse in to bulk out the filling, if you're not going for low carb. I personally love pearl barley in this, but quinoa or lentils will do deliciously too!

12. Pork Meatballs(DF, LF)

Categories: DF, LF
Serves: 4
Preparation time: 20 minutes
Ingredients:
20 oz ground pork
2 tablespoons almond flour
1 egg
1 tablespoons soy sauce
½ cup onion

Preparation:

1) Mince the onion and then use your hands to bring it together with the ground pork, egg, almond flour and soy sauce. Season well with salt and pepper.
2) Shape the mixture into 24 roughly evenly sized balls.
3) Set the Instant Pot to Sauté and add in 2 tablespoons of oil when the setting reads Hot.
4) You'll probably only have room to cook half of the meatballs at a time, so place 12 in, and turn them after 2 minutes.
5) Roll them again after another minute, and then, a minute later take them out. This means that total cook time for 1 batch should be less than 5 minutes.
6) Repeat steps 4 and 5 with the second 12 meatballs.

Serving Suggestion: To make a meal of this, serve with a cream sauce, flavoured with a little onion and garlic and using the cooking juice from the meatballs.

Tip: Pork is okay to be eaten a little on the pink side, so don't worry too much about the cooking of the meatballs. In my opinion, it's better they're a little pink the middle and still nice and moist, rather than overcooked and dry.

13. Sausage Casserole(DF, LC)

Categories: DF, LC
Serves: 4
Preparation time: 30 minutes
Ingredients:
28 oz tinned tomatoes
15 oz tomato paste
10 pork sausages
4 bell peppers
3 tablespoons Italian herbs

Preparation:

1) Into your instant pot, add the tinned tomatoes, tomato paste and Italian herbs and 1 cup of water and then mix the sausages in.
2) Chop and de-seed the bell peppers and add them to the pot on top of the sausages but don't mix them in.
3) Select High Pressure for 25 minutes and then quick release the pressure.

Serving Suggestion: Sausage casserole is almost everything you need in one go! All I would suggest is to serve with more veggies to pack the goodness in.

Tip: It is sometimes nice to quickly grill the sausages beforehand, so that you get that little bit of charring on the skin, but it's not necessary.

14. Whole Ham(DF, LC)

Categories: DF, LC
Serves: 4
Preparation time: 20 minutes
Ingredients:
10 cloves
1 whole ham
1 cup pineapple juice
1 cup mustard
½ cup brown sugar

Preparation:

1) Mix together the pineapple juice, mustard and brown sugar.
2) Slice diagonally into the top of the ham, and place the cloves into these gaps.
3) Put the ham into the Instant Pot, and pour the sauce in and around it.
4) Cook on High Pressure for an hour and then naturally release the pressure.
5) Slice the ham and keep the sauce for pouring over the ham when you serve – delicious!

Serving Suggestion: Serve with a mountain of veggies and keep this low carb and delicious!

Tip: Place pineapple rings into the pot too, for that added extra in the sauce.

Poultry Dishes

1. Buffalo Hot Wings(DF, GF, LC)

Categories: DF, GF, LC
Serves: 6
Preparation time: 25 minutes
Ingredients:
64 oz chicken wings
2 tablespoons honey
1 tablespoon Worcestershire sauce
½ cup hot sauce
Fresh spring onions to top

Preparation:

1) Mix the hot sauce together with the Worcestershire sauce and honey, and season with salt to taste.
2) Pour with ¾ of a cup of water into the bottom of your Instant Pot, and then add a rack into there.
3) Place the chicken wings on the rack and cook on High Pressure for 5 minutes.
4) Allow a 5 minutes natural release, and then quick release.
5) Brush the wings generously with the sauce and then place under the broiler for 5 minutes to crisp up the skin.

Serving Suggestion: These are a great dish to take to a buffet party, they're a huge crowd pleaser!

Tip: For extra spice infusion, mix the water in the bottom of the Instant Pot with more hot sauce.

2. Cacciatore Chicken Drumsticks(DF, GF, LC)

Categories: DF, GF, LC
Serves: 4
Preparation time: 30 minutes
Ingredients:
28 oz tinned tomatoes
8 chicken drumsticks
1 onion
1 teaspoon dried oregano
½ cup black olives

Preparation:

1) Set the Instant Pot to Saute and add in a cup of salted water.
2) Dice the onion.
3) Then, add in the chicken, onion, oregano and tinned tomatoes.
4) Cook for 15 minutes on High Pressure and then allow natural release.
5) Check that the chicken is cooked through, and if not, keep cooking it on Saute mode until it is.
6) Chop the olives and stir through the sauce.
7) Season with salt and pepper to taste and enjoy.

Serving Suggestion: A green Italian side salad is all you'll need to enjoy this as a meal.

Tip: To check the chicken without having to cut it open, use a meat thermometer to ensure that the temperature has reached 165F.

3. Cashew Chicken Curry(DF, LC)

Categories: DF, LC
Serves: 4
Preparation time: 20 minutes
Ingredients:
4 chicken breasts
3 tablespoons yellow curry powder
2 cups coconut milk
1 cup unsalted cashews + extra to garnish
1 teaspoon cumin

Preparation:

1) Dice the chicken and put in into the Instant Pot.
2) Mix together the curry powder, cumin and 2 cups of water. Season well with salt, and pour into the pot.
3) Stir in the cashews and coconut milk, and cook everything together on High Pressure for 8 minutes, before allowing a natural release.

Serving Suggestion: Whatever vegetables you have can be chopped up and added into the curry. Then, add a dollop of coconut yoghurt on top, and garnish with additional cashews and fresh cilantro.

Tip: To make your own yellow curry powder (and have some leftover for next time!), try this; into a pan, add 6 whole cloves, 3 tablespoons of coriander seeds, 2 tablespoons of turmeric, 2 tablespoons chilli powder, 2 teaspoons of cumin seeds, 2 teaspoons of white peppercorns, 1 teaspoon of fenugreek seeds, 1 teaspoon of fennel seeds and 1 teaspoon of yellow mustard seeds. Toast all of the spices over a medium heat for 10-12 minutes, until it's wonderfully fragrant. Then, when the spices are cooled, pulse them all together into a powder.

4. Garlic Butter Chicken(GF, LC)

Categories: GF, LC
Serves: 4
Preparation time: 35 minutes
Ingredients:
4 chicken breasts
2 garlic cloves
2 tablespoons butter
1 teaspoon turmeric or curry powder
Pinch of salt

Preparation:

1) Place the 4 chicken breasts into your Instant Pot.
2) Add in 2 tablespoons of butter.
3) Mince the garlic cloves and add them in too.
4) Sprinkle in a teaspoon of turmeric or curry powder and season with a dash of salt.
5) Set the timer on the Instant Pot for 35 minutes, and then pay attention to follow the instructions for releasing the pressure.
6) Once the chicken is cooked, use 2 forks to shred it whilst it's still in the pot to mix the flavours around more. Enjoy!

Serving Suggestion: Make this into a full meal by serving with wilted spinach and almond salad.

Tip: If you find that your chicken has dried out a little by the time you come to serve it, just stir another tablespoonful of butter through it.

5. Maple Dijon Chicken Wings(DF, LC, LF)

Categories: DF, LC, LF
Serves: 4
Preparation time: 20 minutes
Ingredients:
48 oz chicken wings
2 tablespoons Dijon mustard
2 tablespoons soy sauce
1 tablespoon apple cider vinegar
1/3 cup maple syrup

Preparation:

1) Whisk the Dijon mustard, soy sauce, apple cider vinegar and maple syrup together in the Instant Pot until smooth.
2) Add the chicken wings into the pot and toss well to coat them in the sauce.
3) Set the pressure to High for 10 minutes. Then, Quick Release the pressure.
4) Set the Instant Pot to Saute and reduce the sauce down to your desired consistency.

Serving Suggestion: Keep this healthy by serving on a huge bed of salad. Spinach would be awesome.

Tip: If you want crispy skin on your wings, stick them under the grill for 3-4 minutes.

6. Perfect Turkey Breast(DF, GF, LC, LF)

Categories: DF, GF, LC, LF
Serves: 4-6
Preparation time: 30 minutes
Ingredients:
64 oz turkey breast
2 sticks celery
1 ½ cups turkey broth (or chicken broth)
1 tablespoon onion powder
1 teaspoon garlic powder

Preparation:

1) Dice the celery.
2) Pour the broth into the bottom of the pot, and add in the celery.
3) Place in the steaming rack and put the turkey breast pieces onto it. Sprinkle the onion and garlic powder onto the breasts.
4) Set the pot to High Pressure for 25 minutes. Then, naturally release the pressure for 10 minutes, before quick releasing the rest.

Serving Suggestion: I can't tell you how to have your turkey breast! All I'm saying is that personally, I would serve it with chestnut and sage stuffing, wilted spinach and a delicious gravy.

Tip: Use a meat thermometer to check if the turkey's done, if you're not sure. It should read 165F. If it doesn't, simply cook the turkey for another few minutes until it reaches temperature.

7. Perfectly Poached Chicken Breasts(DF, GF, LC, LF)

Categories: DF, GF, LC, LF
Serves: 4
Preparation time: 15 minutes
Ingredients:
4 chicken breasts
4 cups chicken stock
4 tablespoons fresh parsley
2 garlic cloves
1 onion

Preparation:

1) Peel and chop the onion, roughly chop the parsley and mince the garlic.
2) Add them all into the bottom of your Instant Pot.
3) Add in the chicken breasts, and pour the 4 cups of chicken stock over the top.
4) Set the pot to High Pressure for 10 minutes, and then Quick Release the steam.

Serving Suggestion: A perfectly cooked chicken breast has a whole world of possibilities! Let me set out a few for low carb options for you; chicken salad, chicken and steamed veggies, chicken 'roast' with chestnut stuffing and veg, chicken soup...

Tip: Strain the stock and save it for use again! It will only have got more deliciously chicken-y!

8. Pina Colada Chicken(DF, GF, LC)

Categories: DF, GF, LC
Serves: 4
Preparation time: 45 minutes
Ingredients:
32 oz skinless chicken breast
2 tablespoons coconut oil
1 cup pineapple chunks
½ cup coconut cream
½ cup green onion

Preparation:

1) Chop the chicken into small chunks, and add the bits into the Instant Pot.
2) Then, add in the coconut oil, pineapple chunks and coconut cream.
3) Set the Instant Pot to Poultry and cook for 15 minutes,
4) Allow the pressure to naturally release for 10 minutes and then Quick Release any remaining pressure.
5) Season the sauce with salt and pepper to taste and switch the pot to Saute. Cook for a further 5 minutes, or until the sauce thickens to your liking.
6) Garnish with the green onions and enjoy!

Serving Suggestion: A fresh slaw would be a delicious and summery accompaniment.

Tip: If you would like your sauce to be thicker, you can stir in a tablespoon of arrowroot or starch during the Saute stage.

9. Pollo Guisado(DF, GF, LC, LF)

Categories: DF, GF, LC, LF
Serves: 4
Preparation time: 30 minutes
Ingredients:
8 skinless pieces of chicken (drumsticks or thighs are best)
8 oz canned tomatoes
2 garlic cloves
1 onion
¼ cup cilantro + extra to garnish

Preparation:

1) Mince one of the garlic cloves and mix it with salt. Rub this mix over the chicken.
2) Set the Instant Pot to Saute and add 1 tablespoon of oil. Peel and dice the onion and mince the second garlic cloves. Add them into the pot to begin browning.
3) After 2-3 minutes, add in the cilantro for a minute.
4) Then, pour in the canned tomatoes along with 1 ½ cups of water. Also, place in the chicken.
5) Cook on High Pressure for 20 minutes, and then naturally release the steam. Top with fresh cilantro to serve and enjoy.

Serving Suggestion: Add in some extra veggies to bulk this out into a hearty meal.

Tip: For even more flavour, replace the water with chicken stock.

10. Sesame Chicken(DF, GF, LC, LF)

Categories: DF, GF, LC, LF
Serves: 4
Preparation time: 15 minutes
Ingredients:
24 oz boneless chicken
1 tablespoon minced garlic
1 tablespoon sesame seeds
¼ cup honey
1/4 cup soy sauce

Preparation:
1) Add a little amount of oil into the bottom of the Instant Pot and set to sauté.
2) Chop the chicken and begin browning it, for 3-4 minutes, stirring to ensure it's even on all sides.
3) Whisk together the garlic, honey, sesame seeds and soy sauce.
4) Add the sauce into the pot and stir to coat the chicken in it.
5) Set the pout to Poultry and set for 4 minutes. Quick release the pressure and enjoy.

Serving Suggestion: Make some rice in your Instant Pot too and you have a healthy and delicious no hassle dinner all ready to go!

Tip: Because the sauce is so flavoursome, you can use chicken thigh in this dish, which tends to be cheaper than breast.

11. Sticky Moroccan Chicken(DF, GF, LC)

Categories: DF, GF, LC
Serves: 4
Preparation time: 30 minutes
Ingredients:
8-12 chicken drumsticks
4 teaspoons molasses
1 lemon
1 teaspoon fresh ginger
½ cup honey

Preparation:

1) Mince the ginger and mix it together with some salt and pepper. Rub this mix over the chicken drumsticks.
2) Set the Instant Pot to Saute and add in about a tablespoon of oil. Put the chicken into the pot and brown them all over to make a nice, crispy skin.
3) Add in 1 cup of water and set to Low Pressure for 10 minutes. Then, Quick Release the pressure so as to not overcook the chicken.
4) Remove the chicken drumsticks and set aside. Cover them with foil.
5) Keep the juices in the pot and set it to Saute again.
6) Whisk together the honey, fresh ginger and the juice of the lemon.
7) When the cooking juices have boiled, add the honey mixture in and bring it to a slow boil. Reduce the sauce down for 10-15 minutes, until it's thick and glossy.
8) Coat the drumsticks with the sauce and enjoy!

Serving Suggestion: A fresh and herby Moroccan salad wouldn't go amiss!

Tip: If you let the sauce reduce too much, you can stir in a little bit of water to thin it out again.

12. Turkey Pizza Casserole(GF, LC)

Categories: GF, LC
Serves: 4-6
Preparation time: 15 minutes
Ingredients:
16 oz ground turkey
2 cups crushed tomatoes
2 garlic cloves
1 cup cheese (a mix of cheddar and mozzarella is great to make it really pizza-y)
1 tablespoon oregano

Preparation:

1) Mince the garlic.
2) Mix the garlic together with the tomatoes and oregano, and season well with salt and pepper.
3) Into the bottom of the Instant Pot, add ¼ of the tomato mixture.
4) Then, add on top ¼ of the ground turkey and ¼ of the cheese.
5) Repeat this layering mixture 4 times until you are out of ingredients.
6) Cook on High Pressure for 6 minutes, and then allow it to naturally release.

Serving Suggestion: Maybe Friday night used to be pizza night, but now you've gone low carb. Well, Friday night can be pizza night once more now with this beauty of a dish!

Tip: Well, everyone has their own way of enjoying pizza, right? So add in whatever are your own personal favourite toppings.

13. Whole Chicken(DF, GF, LC, LF)

Categories: DF, GF, LC, LF
Serves: 4-6
Preparation time: 40 minutes
Ingredients:
1 ½ cups chicken broth
1 ½ teaspoons oregano
1 whole chicken
1 teaspoons garlic salt

Preparation:

1) Put the Instant Pot to Saute and add in 2 tablespoons of olive oil. Add the chicken in to cook for 2 minutes on each side.
2) Rub the oregano and garlic salt into the chicken skin.
3) Add in the chicken broth and set in a rack to have the chicken sitting just into the broth.
4) Steam for 25 minutes and then naturally release the pressure.

Serving Suggestion: Steam up a storm of veggies and enjoy a healthy and delicious dinner!

Tip: Whatever flavours you like on your chicken are good! Switch out the oregano and garlic salt for whatever you prefer!

14. Whole Crispy Duck(DF, GF, LC)

Categories: DF, GF, LC
Serves: 4
Preparation time: 60 minutes
Ingredients:
8 carrots
4 garlic cloves
2 tablespoons barbecue rub
1 onion
1 whole duck

Preparation:

1) Quarter the duck.
2) Mix the barbecue rub with salt and pepper, and season all 4 pieces of the duck.
3) Peel and roughly chop the carrots, and line the bottom of the Instant Pot with them.
4) Mince the garlic, and peel and slice the onion. Sprinkle these both all over the carrots.
5) Pour in ½ a cup of water, and place the duck on top of the vegetables. Cook on High Pressure for 25 minutes and then allow it to naturally release.
6) Take everything out of the Instant Pot, and then set it to Saute. Place the duck in, skin side down and leave the skin for 5-10 minutes to crisp up.
7) Serve the dusk with the carrots and enjoy!

Serving Suggestion: Leafy greens are a duck's best friend! (You've heard that one before right?)

Tip: If you'd like to make your own barbecue rub, here's how! Simply mix together ½ a cup of brown sugar, ½ a cup of paprika, 1 tablespoon of chilli powder, 1 tablespoon of garlic powder, 1 tablespoon of onion powder, 1 teaspoon of cayenne pepper, and a good amount of salt and black pepper. This will make more than you need for the recipe, so store it in an airtight container and enjoy this dish over and over again!

Seafood Dishes

1. Asian Salmon Fillets(DF, GF, LC, LF)

Categories: DF, GF, LC, LF
Serves: 2
Preparation time: 15 minutes
Ingredients:
2 frozen salmon fillets
2 tablespoons honey
1 ½ tablespoons brown sugar
1 teaspoon sesame seeds
¼ teaspoon ginger

Preparation:

1) Add the brown sugar into the Instant Pot, along with 1 tablespoon of oil. Stir until the sugar has melted.
2) Then, add in the ginger and honey and mix everything together.
3) Place the salmon fillets in, skin side up, if they have skin on and cook on Low Pressure for 2 minutes.
4) Allow 5 minutes of natural pressure release, and then scoop the salmon out of the pot.
5) Ladle some of the broth over it too, and sprinkle with sesame seeds.

Serving Suggestion: Serve on a bed of wilted Asian greens.

Tip: Add chilli if you like it spicy!

2. Chilli & Lime Salmon(DF, GF, LC, LF)

Categories: DF, GF, LC, LF
Serves: 4
Preparation time: 20 minutes
Ingredients:
4 salmon fillets
2 garlic cloves
1 jalapeno
1 lime
1 tablespoon honey

Preparation:

1) De-seed and dice the jalapeno, juice the lime and mince the garlic.
2) Mix them all together, along with the honey, and a tablespoon of hot water to bring everything together.
3) Into the bottom of the Instant Pot, pour 1 cup of water, and add in the steaming rack.
4) Season the salmon with salt and pepper, and place onto the steaming rack.
5) Steam the salmon for 5 minutes on High Pressure, and then do a quick release.
6) Season the sauce to taste and serve drizzled over the salmon.

Serving Suggestion: Crispy kale and bacon as a side for this is absolute perfection!

Tip: It's easier (and lower in fat!) if you have skinless salmon. If you're a sucker for a crispy salmon skin, though, you can place the salmon skin side down in the Instant Pot on Saute for just a minute or 2 after the steaming.

3. Cod with Cherry Tomatoes(GF, LC)

Categories: GF, LC
Serves: 2
Preparation time: 40 minutes
Ingredients:
2 tablespoons butter
1 large cod fillet
1 cup cherry tomatoes
1 garlic clove

Preparation:

1) Add the cup of tomatoes to a Pyrex dish that will fit into your Instant Pot.
2) Chop your large fillet in half and place the 2 halves on top of the tomatoes.
3) Season with salt and pepper.
4) Mince the garlic and stir it into your butter. Then, place a tablespoon of garlic butter onto each piece of cod.
5) Pour 1 cup into the bottom of the Instant Pot, and place in the steam rack.
6) Place your dish of cod on top of the rack and set to High Pressure for 5 minutes. Naturally release the pressure and enjoy.

Serving Suggestion: Serve with steamed greens to keep it fresh and low carb and all-round yummy!

Tip: You can make this dish from frozen cod just as easily. Just set the pot on for 9 minutes instead of 5.

4. Lobster Tails(GF, LC)

Categories: GF, LC
Serves: 6
Preparation time: 10 minutes
Ingredients:
32 oz lobster tails
½ cup butter

Preparation:

1) Place a steaming rack into your Instant Pot, and pour in 1 cup of water.
2) Chop your lobster tails in half, to expose the meat. Place the tails, shell side down on the steaming rack in the Instant Pot.
3) Steam for 3 minutes on High Pressure, and then do a Quick Release.
4) Season the cooked tails with salt, and serve each with a knob of melting butter.

Serving Suggestion: Lobster tails are so fresh that it would be a crime to serve them with something heavy! A fresh, and maybe slightly spicy salad (I'm talking onion, radish etc) would be perfect.

Tip: If you aren't into eating the lobster on its own, this is still a great way to cook the lobster first, before making it into whatever other dish you like, such as fish cakes, for example, or mac & cheese!

5. Louisiana Shrimp(LC)

Categories: LC
Serves: 4
Preparation time: 10 minutes
Ingredients:
16 oz raw shrimp, in shells
2 garlic cloves
1 lemon
1 teaspoon Louisiana seasoning
½ cup butter

Preparation:

1) Zest and juice the lemon.
2) Ensure that the shrimp are all de-veined.
3) Lightly oil the bottom of the Instant Pot.
4) Into the Instant Pot, put the shrimp, Louisiana seasoning and lemon juice. Also, mince in the garlic.
5) Slice the butter and put it on top of the shrimp.
6) Cook on High Pressure for 2 minutes, and then Quick Release the pressure. Serve immediately.

Serving Suggestion: Use this shrimp to jazz up a boring salad and you're onto a winner!

Tip: To make your own Louisiana seasoning, combine 2 tablespoons of bay leaf powder, 2 tablespoons of celery salt, 2 teaspoons of ground black pepper, 2 teaspoons of ground ginger, 2 teaspoons of smoked paprika, 1 tablespoon of dry mustard, 1 teaspoon of white pepper, 1 teaspoon of ground cinnamon, 1 teaspoon of ground nutmeg, 1 teaspoon of ground cloves, 1 teaspoon of ground allspice, ½ a teaspoon of crushed red pepper flaked, ½ a teaspoon of mace and ½ a teaspoon of ground cardamom.

6. Mussels in Garlic Sauce(GF, LC)

Categories: GF, LC
Serves: 4
Preparation time: 15 minutes
Ingredients:
48 oz mussels
4 garlic cloves
2 tablespoons heavy cream
1 large red bell pepper
¾ cup fish stock

Preparation:

1) Scrub and de-beard the mussels if necessary.
2) Set the Instant Pot to Saute and mince the garlic into it, along with a little oil.
3) Slice and de-seed the pepper and add it into the pot.
4) Pour in the fish stock, and ½ a cup of water.
5) Add the mussels to the pot and cook on High Pressure for just 1 minute. Quick Release the pressure.
6) If the mussels haven't opened, steam them for another minute until they do, but without the lid on.
7) Stir the cream through the cooking liquid and enjoy!

Serving Suggestion: Serve with toasted low carb nut bread with garlic and parsley butter for a sophisticated dinner

Tip: If any of the mussels haven't opened, discard them as they're bad!

7. Orange & Ginger Salmon(DF, LC, LF)

Categories: DF, LC, LF
Serves: 4
Preparation time: 40 minutes
Ingredients:
4 salmon fillets
2 garlic cloves
2 tablespoons low sugar orange marmalade
2 teaspoons minced ginger
1 tablespoon soy sauce

Preparation:

1) Put the salmon fillets into a Ziploc bag.
2) Mince the garlic and stir it together with the marmalade, ginger and soy sauce.
3) Pour the sauce into the bag and seal it. Shake well to coat the salmon, and leave it for 15-20 minutes to marinate.
4) Put 2 cups of water into the Instant Pot and add a steaming rack in.
5) Put the bag of salmon onto the rack and cook for 3 minutes on Low Pressure.
6) Natural release the pressure for 5 minutes, and then quick release the rest.
7) If you like, place the salmon under the grill now for 3-5 minutes for a more browned fish.

Serving Suggestion: Serve on a bed of 'spaghetti' made of spiralised vegetables, which can also be steam cooked in your Instant Pot.

Tip: Frozen fish will not marinate so well, so for best results, use fresh fillets.

8. **Salmon & Broccoli(DF, GF, LC, LF)**

Categories: DF, GF, LC, LF
Serves: 2
Preparation time: 35 minutes
Ingredients:
5 oz salmon
5 oz broccoli
½ cup fresh herbs of your choice

Preparation:

1) Pour 5 ½ fl oz of water into the bottom of the Instant Pot.
2) Chop the broccoli into florets and add it into the steaming basket along with the salmon.
3) Season with salt and pepper and place the basket into the pot. Sprinkle the fresh herbs on top too.
4) Steam for 2 minutes and then naturally release the pressure.

Serving Suggestion: This is a meal all by itself, but just serve with as much extra salad as you like!

Tip: Having a super simple meal is great, but just ensure that you season it well enough for it to taste incredible too.

9. Shrimp & Pea Risotto(GF)

Categories: GF
Serves: 4-6
Preparation time: 15 minutes
Ingredients:
16 oz raw frozen shrimp
2 tablespoons butter
1 cup rice
1 cup frozen peas
1 tablespoon lemon juice

Preparation:

1) Melt the butter into the bottom of the Instant Pot, and then add in the rice, lemon juice and 1 cup of water. Season with salt and pepper.
2) Place the frozen peas and shrimp on top.
3) Cook on High Pressure and then quick release it.
4) If necessary, let it sit for a few minutes to allow the water to absorb in, and then serve.

Serving Suggestion: Risotto is a dish that can stand on its own feet, but why not relax with a nice glass of white wine to compliment your seafood.

Tip: We do need to use frozen peas and shrimp with this, so that they don't overcook in the time it takes for the rice to cook.

10. Shrimp Wontons(DF, LF)

Categories: DF, LF
Serves: 6
Preparation time: 25 minutes
Ingredients:
36 wonton wrappers
12 oz shrimp
2 garlic cloves
1 tablespoons minced ginger
¼ cup Teriyaki sauce

Preparation:

1) Peel and de-vein the shrimp, and chop off the heads.
2) Set the Instant pot to Saute and add in the shrimp for 3-4 minutes to cook through.
3) Then, mince in the garlic, and stir in the ginger too.
4) Transfer everything into a bowl and stir in the Teriyaki sauce. Season with salt to taste.
5) Add 1 tablespoon of filling into the middle of each wonton wrapper. Then, brush the edges with water and fold into a triangle, pressing the edges closed with your fingers. Repeat until you're out of filling!
6) Pour 1 cup of water into the bottom of the Instant Pot, and add in a steaming rack.
7) Place as many wontons as you can onto the steam rack, without layering them.
8) Set to High Pressure for 4 minutes, and then quick release the pressure.
9) Keep repeating until you've cooked all of your wontons! Be sure to top up the water level if it's steamed away!

Serving Suggestion: Serve with fresh green onions on top for a quick flavour and freshness hit.

Tip: You can also make use a mixture of pork and shrimp in the wontons for the more carnivorous among us!

11. Tuna Pasta(DF, LC, LF)

Categories: DF, LC, LF
Serves: 4
Preparation time: 40 minutes
Ingredients:
15 oz canned tomatoes
3 ½ oz canned tuna
2 cups pasta
2 garlic cloves
2 teaspoons dried basil or oregano

Preparation:

1) Set the Instant pot to Saute and mince in the garlic with some oil to begin cooking.
2) Add in the pasta and tomatoes.
3) Stir in the dried herbs.
4) Add in around 1 cup of water, maybe a little more, until the liquid has just covered the top of the pasta.
5) Set to High Pressure for 6 minutes and then naturally release.
6) Drain the tuna and stir it through the pasta.

Serving Suggestion: Make it spicy if you like by adding some chilli to the mix!

Tip: For a more flavoursome sauce, add in half a cup of red wine, and half a cup of water, instead of the full cup of water.

Vegetarian Dishes

1. Asparagus Risotto(DF, GF, LF, V)

Categories: DF, GF, LF, V
Serves: 4
Preparation time: 30 minutes
Ingredients:
16 oz asparagus
2 cups Arborio rice
1 red onion
½ teaspoon lemon juice
¼ cup dry white wine

Preparation:

1) Trim the woody stems off of the asparagus and wash it. Dice the rest of it.
2) Add the stems into the Instant Pot with 4 cups of water. Cook for 12 minutes at High Pressure. Release all of the pressure through the valve.
3) Discard the stems of the asparagus, but keep the cooking liquid and set aside.
4) Keep the pot hot. Dice the onion and add them into the pot with a little oil to begin to soften.
5) Add in the rice and stir everything well for about 2 minutes.
6) Pour the wine in, and when it's evaporated, add the cooking liquid back in, as well as the diced asparagus.
7) Once everything is well mixed, cook for 6 minutes on High Pressure, and then do a quick release.
8) Finally, stir the lemon juice through, season with salt and pepper and enjoy.

Serving Suggestion: Pair with a glass of dry white wine (maybe even the same one you cooked with!) and enjoy a romantic candlelit dinner for 2?

Tip: Risotto is supposed to be sticky and moist, so don't worry if it looks like the liquid hasn't cooked out – it isn't supposed to!

2. Barbecue Pulled Cabbage(DF, GF, LF, V)

Categories: DF, GF, LF, V
Serves: 6
Preparation time: 15 minutes
Ingredients:
2 ½ cups barbecue sauce
1 cabbage
1 onion
Hot sauce (optional)

Preparation:

1) Set the Instant Pot to Sauté, and then add 2 tablespoons of water in, once it's reached Hot.
2) Shred the cabbage and chop the onion and add them into the pot.
3) Sauté for 4-5 minutes, until you see the cabbage begin to soften, and then stir in the barbecue sauce. Also, add the hot sauce if you've chosen to use it.
4) Mix everything together, and allow it to heat through for another 3 minutes or so, and then enjoy!

Serving Suggestion: Serve it 'pulled pork style' in soft, white buns, and with fresh chips and salad on the side – it's perfection!

Tip: If you prefer, of course, you can make your own barbecue sauce. Mix together ¾ of a cup of ketchup with 1 tablespoons white wine vinegar, 1 tablespoon Worcestershire sauce, 2 tablespoons brown sugar and 2 teaspoons paprika. Adjust the seasoning to taste, and then double the quantities for this recipe.

3. Cannellini & Mint Salad(DF, GF, LC, V)

Categories: DF, GF, LC, V
Serves: 4
Preparation time: 15 minutes
Ingredients:
1 cup cannellini beans
1 garlic clove
1 bay leaf
1 sprig fresh mint
Squeeze of lemon juice

Preparation:

1) Soak the cannellini beans overnight.
2) Pour 4 cups of water into the Instant Pot, and then add in the soaked beans and bay leaf. Mince the garlic and add it in too.
3) Set the pot to High Pressure on 8 minutes.
4) Naturally release the pressure and then drain the beans and remove the bay leaf.
5) Stir through the mint leaves, and season with salt, pepper and oil

Serving Suggestion: Use this as a base for a bigger salad. Use it to top whatever other veggies you want!

Tip: The beans only need to be soaked for 5 hours, but we recommend overnight so you can just go to bed and forget about it!

4. Coconut Lime Quinoa(DF, GF, LF, V)

Categories: DF, GF, LF, V
Serves: 6
Preparation time: 20 minutes
Ingredients:
14 oz coconut milk
1 cup quinoa
1 lime

Preparation:

1) Rinse the quinoa.
2) Into your Instant Pot, add the quinoa, coconut milk, a pinch of salt and ¼ cup of water.
3) Cook on High Pressure for just 1 minute, and then allow the pressure to natural release for another 10 minutes.
4) Zest and juice the lime, and stir as much as you want through the quinoa whilst fluffing it up before serving.

Serving Suggestion: If you don't have a very sweet tooth, this is a great healthy breakfast idea.

Tip: Really do only cook the quinoa for a minute, as the water will be absorbed very quickly and otherwise you may get sticking.

5. Eggplant Stew(DF, GF, LV, V)

Categories: DF, GF, LV, V
Serves: 6
Preparation time: 10 minutes
Ingredients:
28 oz canned tomatoes
16 oz eggplant
2 garlic cloves
1 onion
½ teaspoon ground coriander

Preparation:

1) Dice your eggplant.
2) Add the eggplant into the Instant Pot, along with the tomatoes and 1 cup of water.
3) Peel and slice the onion, and mince the garlic and add them both into the pot too.
4) Season well with salt and pepper, and stir in the coriander.
5) Steam on High Pressure for 4 minutes and then Quick Release the pressure. Enjoy!

Serving Suggestion: Keep it middle-eastern and serve with lentils.

Tip: Normally, naturally releasing the pressure is great, but since the stew is almost entirely make of eggplant, leaving it in there will result in most or a mush!

6. Frittata(DF,GF, LC)

Categories: DF,GF, LC
Serves: 6
Preparation time: 20 minutes
Ingredients:
6 eggs
1 cup spinach
¼ cup tomato
¼ cup onion
Pinch of salt

Preparation:

1) Dice the onion and tomato.
2) Grease a pan to fit inside your Instant Pot. Add 1 cup of water into the bottom of the pot and then stack the pan inside on top of the rack.
3) Crack the eggs and beat lightly. Then, stir in the spinach, tomato, onion and a good pinch of salt.
4) Pour the egg mixture into the pan and select 5 minutes of pressure cooking, and then allow a slow release for 10 minutes.

Serving Suggestion: This is a healthy and nutritious breakfast to keep you full until lunchtime!

Tip: Throw in any vegetables you have around! If you add potatoes in, you'll need to increase the cook time to 20 minutes.

7. Garlic & Sage Spaghetti Squash(DF, GF, LC, LF, V)

Categories: DF, GF, LC, LF, V
Serves: 2
Preparation time: 10 minutes
Ingredients:
5 garlic cloves
2 tablespoons olive oil
1 medium spaghetti squash
½ cup fresh sage leaves
¼ teaspoon nutmeg

Preparation:

1) Set the Instant Pot to Saute and add in the olive oil and sage leaves. Also, mince in the garlic.
2) Stir occasionally, until the sage leaves have turned crispy. Then, set the sauce aside.
3) Chop the squash in half and scoop out the seeds.
4) Add 1 cup of water into the Instant Pot, and put in the 2 spaghetti squash halves. Ensure that they are skin side down.
5) Cook for 3 minutes at High Pressure, and then do a Quick Release
6) Use a fork to tease the strands out of the spaghetti squash, and stir them through the sauce.
7) Sprinkle on the nutmeg and season with salt and then enjoy!

Serving Suggestion: You literally don't need anything else with this dish! It's a delicious spaghetti dinner all by itself! If you want though, a side salad is never a bad idea.

Tip: If the strands don't seem to be coming out very easily, just cook the squash for another minute. Be careful, as it can very quickly just turn to mush!

8. GF Broccoli & Cheddar Pasta(GF)

Categories: GF
Serves: 8-12
Preparation time: 30 minutes
Ingredients:
16 oz gluten-free pasta (wholemeal if you have it)
8 oz grated cheddar cheese
1 cup frozen broccoli
1 cup milk

Preparation:

1) Put the pasta into your Instant Pot and add 4 cups of water.
2) Add a steamer into the pot and put the frozen broccoli into it.
3) Cook on High Pressure for 4 minutes and then quick release the pressure.
4) Change the setting to Sauté and stir in the broccoli, and then the milk and cheese until the cheese is melted and serve hot.

Serving Suggestion: Well, we weren't going for low carb on this recipe anyway, were we, so why not serve with fresh bread?

Tip: Using wholemeal pasta is a great way to get fibre into your diet.

9. Hummus(DF, GF, LF, V)

Categories: DF, GF, LF, V
Serves: 4
Preparation time: 15 minutes
Ingredients:
14 oz dried garbanzo beans
2 cloves garlic
1 lemon
¼ cup olive oil
¼ cup taihini

Preparation:

1) Rinse the garbanzo beans and take care to remove any stones.
2) Place the beans into the Instant Pot along with 12 cups of water. Set to Manual for 35 minutes.
3) Allow the pressure to naturally release, and then drain the beans but preserve the liquid still.
4) Add the beans into a food processor, along with ½ a cup of the cooking liquid, the garlic and taihini.
5) Process until smooth and then add in the olive oil, 1 tablespoon at a time.

Serving Suggestion: This is a healthy lunch choice when you serve it with chopped, raw vegetables.

Tip: Add in herbs and spices if you want a different flavour in your hummus.

10. Mushroom Pate(DF, GF, LC, LF, V)

Categories: DF, GF, LC, LF, V
Serves: 4-6
Preparation time: 30 minutes
Ingredients:
16 oz button mushrooms
1 shallot
1 bay leaf
¾ cup porcini mushrooms
¼ cup dry white wine

Preparation:

1) Add 1 cup of water over the porcini mushrooms. Cover the dish and set aside.
2) Set the Instant Pot to Sauté and add in a little oil when it reads Hot.
3) Chop the shallot and begin sautéing it.
4) Slice the button mushrooms and add them in too to begin to brown.
5) Then, pour in the wine and let it evaporate.
6) Then, add the porcini, including their soaking liquid.
7) Season with salt and pepper and add in the bay leaf.
8) Set the Instant Pot to 12 minutes of pressure cooking and then quick release the pressure.
9) Discard the bay leaf and puree the contents of the pot to the consistency you like.

Serving Suggestion: Serve on low carb nut and seed crackers for an enjoyable lunch.

Tip: If porcini mushrooms are not easily accessible for you, substitute in a different variety of fresh mushroom, and just add them in with the button mushrooms.

11. Spiced Cauliflower Steaks(DF, GF, LC, LF, V)

Categories: DF, GF, LC, LF, V
Serves: 4-6
Preparation time: 15 minutes
Ingredients:
2 large cauliflowers
2 teaspoons paprika
2 teaspoons cumin
1 cup fresh cilantro

Preparation:
1) Set the Instant Pot to Steam and add in 1 ½ cups of water. Place a rack inside the pot.
2) Remove the leaves from the cauliflower and cut each one in half. Trim them so that they can sit flat on the rack.
3) Mix the paprika and cumin together with a pinch of salt and a little oil.
4) Drizzle the mixture over the cauliflower and rub it in.
5) Place the cauliflower steaks onto the rack and cook for 4 minutes, then quick releasing the pressure.
6) Cut the cooked cauliflower in 1 ½ inch thick steaks and sprinkle with fresh cilantro to serve.

Serving Suggestion: Make a whole load of steamed veggies in your Instant Pot to serve beside these steaks and have a low carb, low fat meal just packed full of goodness!

Tip: If your Instant Pot is big enough for 2 racks, you can steam other veggies underneath the cauliflower at the same time. Just add in ½ a cup more water and give the steaks an extra minute or so of cooking time.

12. Spinach & Artichoke Dip(GF, LC, V)

Categories: GF, LC, V
Serves: 4
Preparation time: 20 minutes
Ingredients:
14 oz canned artichoke hearts
10 oz frozen spinach
1 cup Parmesan
1 cup sour cream
1 cup mozzarella

Preparation:

1) Shred the mozzarella and mix it together with the sour cream and parmesan.
2) Drain any excess water from the spinach and drain the artichoke hearts. Stir them through the mixture too. Season with salt and pepper to taste.
3) Lightly grease a baking dish that will fit into your Instant Pot.
4) Pour 2 cups of water into the bottom of the Instant Pot and add in the steaming rack.
5) Place the dish onto the steaming rack and cook at High Pressure for 10 minutes. Then, quick release the pressure.

Serving Suggestion: Dip in strips of veggies for a tasty and delicious snack.

Tip: If you want a crispy cheese top, reserve some of the cheese and sprinkle it on top after the cooking is done. Then, place the dish under the grill until you've got your desired effect.

13. Spinach Daal(DF, GF, LF, V)

Categories: DF, GF, LF, V
Serves: 4
Preparation time: 25 minutes
Ingredients:
4 garlic cloves
2 cups spinach
2 plum tomatoes
1 cup lentils
1 teaspoon cumin seeds

Preparation:

1) Set your Instant Pot to Saute and Hot, and add in a little oil. Then add in the cumin seeds.
2) Mince the garlic and stir it in too.
3) Once the garlic is fragrant, dice the tomatoes and add them in, along with the lentils and 2 cups of water and stir everything around.
4) Set the pot to High Pressure for 5 minutes. Then, naturally release the steam for 5 minutes and then quick release the rest.
5) Add up to another 2 cups of water to bring the lentils to your desired consistency.
6) Then, blend the mixture until smooth.
7) Roughly chop the spinach leaves and stir them through the daal, whilst it's still hot.
8) Set the pot back to Saute and bring the mixture to a gentle boil.
9) Season with salt to taste and enjoy!

Serving Suggestion: Naan bread!

Tip: The texture of daals can vary a lot. For this meal, since we're not serving with rice, we like to keep it pretty thick. If you prefer though, add more water in to create a thinner consistency.

Soup Dishes

1. Beetroot Borscht(DF, GF, LC, LF, V)

Categories: DF, GF, LC, LF, V
Serves: 4
Preparation time: 60 minutes
Ingredients:
4 large beetroots
3 cups cabbage
2 carrots
2 bay leaves
1 onion

Preparation:
1) Dice the beetroots, carrots and the onion, and shred the cabbage.
2) Pour 6 cups of water into the Instant Pot, and season well with salt and pepper.
3) Add the bay leaves into the pot, and then add in all of the vegetables.
4) Set the pot onto the Soup setting, and cook for 45 minutes, before allowing a natural release.
5) Remove the bay leaves, season again, if necessary, and enjoy!

Serving Suggestion: A dollop of sour cream on top, and some fresh herbs will take this to the next level!

Tip: If you're looking for a quick and simple way to remove your beetroot skins, try this; Pour 1 cup of water into the Instant Pot and place in a steam rack. Steam the beetroots for 7 minutes, and then Quick Release the pressure. Drop the beetroots straight into an ice bath, and the skins should come right off!

2. Broccoli & Stilton Soup(GF, LC)

Categories: GF, LC
Serves: 4-6
Preparation time: 20 minutes
Ingredients:
5 oz stilton
2 heads broccoli
2 garlic cloves
1 cup red onion
½ cup carrot

Preparation:

1) Set the Instant Pot to Sauté and add a little oil in to lightly coat the bottom of the pot.
2) Whilst it's heating, mince the onion and garlic, and shop the carrot and broccoli.
3) Then, add all of the vegetables into the pot, and season with salt and pepper. Cook for 3 minutes and stir occasionally to avoid sticking.
4) Add in 2 ½ cups of water and set on High Pressure for 4 minutes. Then, Quick Release the steam.
5) Try to scoop out roughly half of the broccoli, and don't worry if other veggies come along with it.
6) Blend the soup in the pot, and stir through the stilton until it's melted in.
7) Stir the broccoli you took out back in and enjoy hot.

Serving Suggestion: Sprinkle some nuts and seeds of your choice on top of your soup to add a little extra texture.

Tip: If you don't like any lumps in your soup then just blend the whole thing!

3. Butternut Squash & Ginger Soup(DF, GF, LF, V)

Categories: DF, GF, LF, V
Serves: 6-8
Preparation time: 25 minutes
Ingredients:
64 oz butternut squash
4 cups vegetable stock
1 onion
1 sprig sage
½ inch piece of ginger

Preparation:
1) Set the Instant Pot to Sauté and preheat until it reads 'Hot'.
2) Peel and dice the onion and butternut squash.
3) Into the Instant Pot, add the onion and sage and season with salt and pepper.
4) Then, add a handful of the chopped squash in to brown.
5) After 5 minutes or so, add in the rest of the squash along with the vegetable stock and the minced ginger.
6) Select 10 minutes on High Pressure, and then use quick release.
7) Remove the sage and blend to your desired consistency.

Serving Suggestion: This soup is awesome and can be frozen! So why not make a big batch and freeze some for an emergency?

Tip: If you like a little more texture, toast some pumpkin seeds and add to the top of the soup when you serve it.

4. Chicken Vegetable Soup(DF, GF, LC, LF)

Categories: DF, GF, LC, LF
Serves: 6
Preparation time: 30 minutes
Ingredients:
64 fl oz chicken broth
16 oz leeks
16 oz chicken breast
16 oz broccoli
6 large carrots

Preparation:

1) Begin heating 2 tablespoons of oil in the Instant Pot on the Saute setting.
2) Dice the chicken into 1 inch pieces, and then add it into the pot to begin browning.
3) Prepare the carrots, leeks and broccoli into small pieces too.
4) Add the vegetable into the pot, along with the broth, and set it to High Pressure for 15 minutes. Then, do a Quick Release.
5) Season with salt and pepper to taste and enjoy!

Serving Suggestion: This soup, because it is unblended, is actually more of a stew. It would also be a delicious filling for a pie! So, why not try your hand at pastry and try making your own chicken vegetable pie with the leftovers?

Tip: This is by no means a '3 veg only' soup. If you have other vegetables, chuck 'em in!

5. Cream of Asparagus Soup(GF, LC)

Categories: GF, LC.
Serves: 4
Preparation time: 25 minutes
Ingredients:
32 oz fresh asparagus
8 oz sour cream
5 cups vegetable broth
2 garlic cloves
1 onion

Preparation:

1) Chop the woody ends off of the asparagus, and then slice the rest into 1 inch pieces. Peel and dice the onion too.
2) Set the Instant Pot to Saute and add in 2 tablespoons of oil. Then, add in the onions for them to begin browning.
3) Mince the garlic into the pot too.
4) After 5 minutes or so, add in 5 cups of vegetable broth, and scrape up any onions or garlic stuck to the bottom of the pan.
5) Add in the chopped asparagus and a good pinch of salt and pepper.
6) Set the pot to High Pressure for 5 minutes. Then, allow the pressure to naturally release for 10 minutes, before quick releasing the rest.
7) Puree the soup, in small batches if necessary, and stir the sour cream through.
8) Season to taste and enjoy!

Serving Suggestion: If you have extra asparagus, just steam it in your Instant Pot and use it to garnish the dish!

Tip: Make this dish dairy free by using coconut milk instead of sour cream.

6. French Onion Soup(GF, LC)

Categories: GF, LC
Serves: 6
Preparation time: At least 18 hours
Ingredients:
48 oz yellow onions
10 cups vegetable broth
2 cups grated Gruyere cheese
2 tablespoons balsamic vinegar
2 tablespoons butter

Preparation:

1) Peel and quarter the onions.
2) Put the onions into the Instant Pot, along with the butter, and season with salt and pepper.
3) Cook on Low Pressure overnight, or for 12 hours.
4) Then, add in the vegetable broth and balsamic vinegar, and cook on Low Pressure for another 6-8 hours.
5) Season again if necessary, and sprinkle 1/3 of a cup of Gruyere on the top of each serving.

Serving Suggestion: It's just delicious! It's all you need on a cold day to warm you up from the inside.

Tip: This soup can really just keep cooking down for days, as long as your pot is retaining moisture! So, don't worry about setting it on one evening and leaving it right until dinner the next evening!

7. Leek & Potato Soup(DF, GF, LF, V)

Categories: DF, GF, LF, V
Serves: 4
Preparation time: 25 minutes
Ingredients:
6 cups vegetable broth
4 potatoes
2 large leeks
Fresh parsley

Preparation:

1) Turn on the Saute function of your Instant Pot and add in 1 tablespoon of oil.
2) Chop the ends off of your leeks, and rinse them. Slice thinly. Then, add the slices into the pot and begin to Saute them.
3) Meanwhile, peel and dice the potatoes.
4) When the leeks are softened, add in the potatoes and vegetable broth.
5) Set the pressure to High for 12 minutes, and then naturally release the pressure.
6) Taste and season with salt and pepper.
7) Chop the fresh parsley and sprinkle on top to garnish.

Serving Suggestion: Soup has to be with fresh bread!

Tip: If you like a thicker soup, you can blend the potatoes into the broth after they're cooked.

8. Lentil Soup(DF, GF, LF, V)

Categories: DF, GF, LF, V
Serves: 4
Preparation time: 25 minutes
Ingredients:
4 cups vegetable broth
2 carrots
1 cup lentils
1 cup frozen spinach
1 garlic clove

Preparation:

1) Choose a pot that can fit inside your Instant Pot. Wash the lentils and put them into that pot.
2) Peel and dice the carrots and mince the garlic, and add them into the pot with the lentils.
3) Add a cup of water to the bottom of the Instant Pot, and then a rack. Put the pot of lentils onto the rack, and pour the vegetable broth into the lentil pot.
4) Set to High Pressure for 15 minutes. Then, allow the pressure to naturally release.
5) Chop the frozen spinach and stir it through the soup.

Serving Suggestion: This could not be more perfect for a cold winter's evening, under a blanket, by the fire, with a hunk of fresh bread, out of a huge mug whilst watching old movies!

Tip: Go ahead and add in any extra veggies too if you like!

9. Minestrone Soup(DF, LF, V)

Categories: DF, LF, V
Serves: 4
Preparation time: 15 minutes
Ingredients:
32 fl oz vegetable stock
14 oz kidney beans
3 carrots
2 stalks celery
1 cup shell pasta

Preparation:

1) Dice the carrots and celery.
2) Place the carrot, celery, pasta, kidney beans and vegetable stock into your Instant Pot.
3) Set to High Pressure for 4 minutes and allow natural release.

Serving Suggestion: Why not make a bigger batch (depending on the size of your Instant Pot, of course!) and have fresh soup for lunch all week?

Tip: You can add in as many other vegetables as you like!

10. Sausage & Kale Soup(DF, GF, LC)

Categories: DF, GF, LC
Serves: 4
Preparation time: 20 minutes
Ingredients:
8 oz sausages
4 cups kale
2 garlic cloves
2 carrots
1 onion

Preparation:

1) Prepare all of the ingredients; chop the kale, slice the sausage, mince the garlic and peel and slice the onion and carrots.
2) Add everything into the Instant Pot, along with 1 cup of water and a seasoning of salt and pepper.
3) Cook on High Pressure for 8 minutes and then Quick Release the steam.
4) Re-season with salt and pepper to taste and enjoy!

Serving Suggestion: A little sprinkling of parmesan is always a great idea on top of a steaming hot bowl of soup.

Tip: As always with vegetables; the more the merrier! Throw in whatever else you have!

11. Spicy Chicken Soup(LC)

Categories: LC
Serves: 4
Preparation time: 30 minutes
Ingredients:
4 chicken breasts
1 cup heavy cream
1 cup diced onion
1 tablespoon ranch dressing
1/3 cup hot sauce

Preparation:
1) Into the Instant Pot, add the chicken, onion, ranch dressing, hot sauce, 2 tablespoons of oil and 3 cups of water.
2) Cook on High Pressure for 10 minutes and then do a Quick Release of the pressure.
3) Take the chicken out of the soup and shred it. Then, add it back in.
4) Stir the cream through, and season with salt and pepper, and more hot sauce if need be, to taste before serving.

Serving Suggestion: Spice is always better the day after. So, why not double up, have some for dinner, and then have plenty of delicious leftovers for lunch the next day? Also, obviously, top with cheese!

Tip: We have used chicken breasts simply for ease, and not having bones to remove, but if you prefer other pieces of chicken, you can use them too.

12. Sweet Potato Coconut Soup(DF, GF, LF, V)

Categories: DF, GF, LF, V
Serves: 4
Preparation time: 60 minutes
Ingredients:
14 fl oz coconut milk
2 garlic cloves
2 large sweet potatoes
2 teaspoons curry powder
1 inch fresh ginger
½ cup red lentils

Preparation:

1) Add a little oil to the bottom of the Instant Pot on Saute function and mine in the garlic and ginger. After a minute, turn it off of Saute.
2) Peel and dice the sweet potatoes and add them in.
3) Rinse the lentils and add them into the pot, along with the curry powder.
4) Add in 4 cups of lightly salted water and then set the pot to High Pressure for 10 minutes, and then do a natural release for 10 minutes, before quick releasing the rest.
5) Blend the soup to your desired consistency (I like a few lumps left in, personally!)
6) Set the pot to Saute and stir in the coconut milk. Once it's mixed in and warmed through, serve!

Serving Suggestion: A whole-meal gluten free roll would dip in perfectly!

Tip: Taste the soup, and add in more curry powder to reach the spice level you like, if necessary!

Side Dishes

1. Apple Sauce(DF, GF, LF, V)

Categories: DF, GF, LF, V
Serves: 8-12
Preparation time: 30 minutes
Ingredients:
48 oz peeled apples and sliced
2 cinnamon sticks
½ teaspoon nutmeg
Honey to taste

Preparation:

1) Add everything into your Instant Pot, along with ¼ cup of water and set to High Pressure for 5 minutes.
2) Natural release the pressure.
3) Remove the cinnamon stick and blend the apple sauce to your desired consistency.
4) Add in salt and honey to taste, if desired.

Serving Suggestion: Apple sauce can be used in place of butter in baking. So, healthy brownies it is!

Tip: Choose your type of apple carefully depending on if you want a sweeter or more tart flavour in your sauce.

2. Baked Potatoes(DF, GF, LF, V)

Categories: DF, GF, LF, V
Serves: 4
Preparation time: 30 minutes
Ingredients:
4 large potatoes
Pinch of salt
Pinch of pepper

Preparation:

1) Stab your potatoes all over with a fork, and sprinkle them with salt and pepper.
2) Add a steaming rack to your Instant Pot and pour in 1 cup of water.
3) Add the potatoes onto the rack and set to pressure cook for 30 minutes.
4) Then, quickly release the steam to avoid over-cooking.

Serving Suggestion: One of the easiest family dinners to do is a baked potatoes with a topping bar. Set out whatever your family's favourite toppings are, and allow them to customise their own dinner.

Tip: Choose potatoes that are pretty much the same size, so that they don't have different cook times.

3. Beetroots with Blue Cheese(GF, LC)

Categories: GF, LC
Serves: 4
Preparation time: 40 minutes
Ingredients:
24 oz beetroots
¼ cup crumbly blue cheese

Preparation:
1) Wash the mud off of the beetroots, and trim of just the leaves.
2) Pour 1 cup of water into the bottom of your Instant Pot and add in the steaming rack.
3) Place the beetroots onto the steaming rack and cook for 24 minutes on High Pressure. Allow the pressure to release naturally.
4) Allow the beetroots to cool enough so that you can handle them, and then pull off the skin from the roots, and trim the ends off.
5) Sprinkle salt and pepper onto the beetroots, and crumble the blue cheese over them whilst they're still warm for some delicious meltiness!

Serving Suggestion: Beetroots are a fantastic cold weather vegetable. Now that you have this quick and easy beetroot side, use it to finish off any dish, or even to make a salad with!

Tip: To begin with, we don't chop off the ends of the beetroot, because you'll just be left with pink juice EVERYWHERE!

4. Bread(DF, LF, V)

Categories: DF, LF, V
Serves: 4
Preparation time: 70 minutes + 2 ½ hours rising + overnight refrigeration
Ingredients:
12 ¼ oz white bread flour
5 ¼ oz rye flour
1 teaspoon olive oil
½ oz dry yeast

Preparation:

1) Mix the flours and the yeast, and then add in the olive oil and up to 9 fl oz of water, a little at a time until a dough takes shape.
2) Knead the dough for 10 minutes, and then leave it to rise in a warm place for an hour.
3) Punch the dough down and refrigerate overnight.
4) The next day, flour a surface and begin pulling and folding the dough. Pull it out, fold it in half and then push down, and repeat. Do this 5 or 6 times until you feel the dough become firmer.
5) Line your Instant Pot with parchment paper along the bottom and halfway up the sides and lay the dough in it. Sprinkle the top with a little extra flour.
6) Set the heat to 85F and leave the pot covered, for the dough to rise for another hour and a half.
7) Then, place the Instant Pot in an over at 465F and cook for 45 minutes.

Serving Suggestion: I can't tell you what to put on your sandwich! What I can tell you is that fresh bread with butter and jam is exquisite.

Tip: So, why make bread in an Instant Pot? The closer proximity of the heat creates a nice, thin crust around the outside, and great, fluffy bread inside.

5. Breakfast Bites(LC)

Categories: LC
Makes: 4
Preparation time: 30 minutes
Ingredients:
4 eggs
4 strips of bacon
1 ½ cups cheddar cheese
½ cup cottage cheese
¼ cup heavy cream

Preparation:

1) Set the Instant Pot to Saute and crisp up your bacon.
2) Pour 1 cup of water into the bottom of the Instant Pot and add in a steaming rack.
3) Crumble up the bacon and sprinkle it into the bottom of 4 ramekins or jars.
4) Blend together the eggs, cheddar, cottage cheese and cream with a pinch of salt and pepper until smooth.
5) Divide the egg mixture evenly between your 4 ramekins.
6) Loosely cover each ramekin with foil and place onto the steam rack in the Instant Pot.
7) Steam on High Pressure for 8 minutes, and then allow the pressure to naturally release for 10 minutes. Quick release any remaining pressure.
8) Remove the ramekins from the pot and allow them to cool a little before turning them out of the pots. Or, just eat straight from the pots!

Serving Suggestion: These can survive in the refrigerator for up to a week, so why not make 2 batches on a Sunday night, and have something great for breakfast all week!

Tip: If you're one of those people who just need the spice, add in a dash of hot sauce to your egg mixture.

6. Cajun Greens(DF, GF, LC)

Categories: DF, GF, LC
Serves: 4
Preparation time: 40 minutes
Ingredients:
16 oz cooked ham
6 cups greens
2 garlic cloves
1 onion
1 turnip

Preparation:

1) Peel and chop the onion and turnip. Mince the garlic.
2) Chop the ham into small pieces.
3) Put the onion, turnip and garlic into the Instant Pot, along with the greens and ham hock.
4) Then, add in 1 tablespoon of oil, ½ of a cup of water and a pinch of salt.
5) Cook for 20 minutes on High Pressure, and then naturally release for 10 minutes.
6) Quick Release any remaining pressure and enjoy!

Serving Suggestion: This is a delicious side dish for a garlic chicken breast, to keep your meal low carb but totally tasty.

Tip: Use whatever your preferred greens are, or a mixture. I personally am a huge spinach fan, but you can also use kale, collard, or any other leaves!

7. Cheesy Polenta(GF)

Categories: GF
Serves: 6
Preparation time: 20 minutes
Ingredients:
4 cups vegetable broth
4 teaspoons butter
1 cup polenta
½ cup grated cheese
¼ cup milk

Preparation:
1) Set the Instant Pot to sauce and whisk the polenta with the chicken broth.
2) Once it begins to boil, change the setting to High Pressure, and seal for 7 minutes.
3) Allow the pressure to release naturally, and then whisk in the butter, cheese and milk.
4) Leave it to rest for 2 minutes, and then enjoy!

Serving Suggestion: This is a delicious side for some oven-roasted veggies.

Tip: If you cannot get vegetarian chicken broth, then you can use vegetable stock instead.

8. Corn on the Cob(DF, LF, V)

Categories: DF, LF, V
Serves: 4
Preparation time: 15 minutes
Ingredients:
4 ears of corn
3 tablespoons soy sauce
1 tablespoon sugar
1 teaspoon garlic powder
¼ teaspoons sesame oil

Preparation:
1) Add 1 cup of cold water into the Instant Pot and then add a rack.
2) Place the ears of corn onto the rack, and cook on High Pressure for 90 seconds, before quick releasing the pressure.
3) Mix together the soy sauce, sugar, garlic powder and sesame oil. Taste and season with salt and pepper if needed.
4) Change the setting to Saute and switch to Hot, after removing any remaining water from the pot.
5) Brush the sauce over the corn, and then cook in the pot for 5-10 minutes until they're reached the level of char that you like. Keep adding more sauce in until it's all used up.

Serving Suggestion: Corn on the cob is one of my favourite side dishes ever! I'd eat it with anything!

Tip: I personally like to get a little light charring (burning!) on my corn, for that extra layer of flavour, but if you don't, just shorten the sauté time!

9. Cranberry Sauce(DF, GF, LF, V)

Categories: DF, GF, LF, V
Serves: 8-12
Preparation time: 25 minutes
Ingredients:
12 oz fresh cranberries
1 cup orange juice
¾ cup sugar
1 cinnamon stick
Zest of 1 orange

Preparation:

1) Add everything into your Instant Pot and set the pressure to High for 6 minutes.
2) Naturally release the pressure for 10 minutes.
3) Set the pot to Sauté and continue cooking for 5 minutes for the sauce to thicken, whilst mashing the sauce to the consistency you like.

Serving Suggestion: Well, it's for a roast dinner, isn't it? This cranberry sauce is sweet enough to also be used in desserts.

Tip: You can reduce the amount of sugar if you prefer a more tart cranberry sauce.

10. Spicy Mac & Cheese(GF)

Categories: GF
Serves: 6
Preparation time: 20 minutes
Ingredients:
16 oz gluten free macaroni
2 cups mature cheddar cheese
1 tablespoon Dijon mustard
½ cup milk
½ teaspoon hot sauce

Preparation:

1) Put the macaroni into your Instant Pot and add 2 ½ cups of salted water. Cook on High Pressure for 5 minutes and then do a Quick Release.
2) Switch the setting to Sauté, and add in the milk, mustard and hot sauce.
3) Then, stir in the cheddar until it has melted.

Serving Suggestion: Garlic bread is always a delicious side dish for mac & cheese

Tip: Taste and add more hot sauce if you handle it!

11. Herby Quinoa(DF, GF, LF, V)

Categories: DF, GF, LF, V
Serves: 4
Preparation time: 15 minutes + overnight soaking
Ingredients:
3 cups vegetable broth
2 cups quinoa
1 cup fresh mixed herbs of your choice
1 lemon

Preparation:

1) Juice the lemon and add 1 tablespoon into a bowl with the quinoa. Ad in water to cover the quinoa and leave it to soak overnight.
2) The next day, into the Instant Pot, pour in the quinoa, remaining lemon juice and the herbs. Season with a little salt and pepper.
3) Pour in 3 cups of vegetable broth and cook on High Pressure for 1 minute.
4) Allow the pressure to naturally release for 10 minutes, and then quick release the rest.

Serving Suggestion: Stir some veggies or salad of your choice through the quinoa for a healthy and filling lunch.

Tip: To know that quinoa is done, look out for it being puffed up, and having the obvious ring around the edge.

12. Maple Mustard Glazed Carrots(LC)

Categories: LC
Serves: 8
Preparation time: 30 minutes
Ingredients:
48 oz carrots
1 tablespoon butter
1 tablespoon maple syrup
1 tablespoon wholegrain mustard
1 teaspoon dried thyme

Preparation:

1) Peel and quarter your carrots.
2) Set the Instant Pot to Saute and add in the butter. Once it's melted, stir in the maple syrup, mustard, thyme and 2 tablespoons of water.
3) Stir everything well, and then add in the carrots and stir them around well to coat.
4) Steam on High Pressure for 4 minutes and then naturally release the pressure for 15 minutes. Quick release any remaining pressure.

Serving Suggestion: Carrots are a great and healthy side to many a meat meal, but can be a little boring. Instead, whip up some of these delicious carrots and enjoy with your chicken.

Tip: Try this recipe with parsnips as well, for a slightly different twist.

13. Popcorn(GF)

Categories: GF
Serves: 4
Preparation time: 10 minutes
Ingredients:
3 tablespoons coconut oil
2 tablespoons butter
½ cup popcorn kernels
Salt

Preparation:

1) Set the Instant Pot to the Saute More setting.
2) Add in the butter and coconut oil to melt down until it's sizzling.
3) Add in the kernels and stri so they're coated with the mixture.
4) Place the lid on the pot and hold it down for 2-3 minutes, until the kernels begin popping.
5) When you see that about 2/3 of the kernels have popped, turn the heat off so that the rest continue popping but you avoid burning.
6) Pour the popcorn into a bowl and sprinkle with a generous amount of salt.

Serving Suggestion: Movie night!

Tip: Don't leave the popcorn sitting in the cooker once it's done, as the bottom will still be hot and so it may begin to burn.

14. Refried Beans(DF, GF, LF, V)

Categories: DF, GF, LF, V
Serves: 6-8
Preparation time: 15 minutes
Ingredients:
2 cups red or black beans
1 bunch fresh cilantro
1 teaspoon vegetable oil
½ cup onion
½ teaspoon chilli powder

Preparation:

1) Set the Instant Pot to Saute and add in the diced onion, cilantro leaves, chilli powder and vegetable oil.
2) Once the onions are softened, add the beans and 2 cups of water.
3) Set to 10 minutes on High Pressure and then allow natural release.
4) Then, sprinkle a little salt on the beans and mash to the desired consistency.

Serving Suggestion: Nachos!

Tip: To make this a pretty dish to serve, take a scoop of beans out before the mashing and use them on top of the dish, and dress it with fresh cilantro too.

15. Rice Pilaf(DF, GF, LF, V)

Categories: DF, GF, LF, V
Serves: 4
Preparation time: 10 minutes
Ingredients:
2 cups vegetable broth
1 cup rice
1 tablespoon coconut oil
¼ cup dried vegetable soup mix

Preparation:
1) Add the coconut oil to the bottom of the Instant Pot.
2) Add the rice into the Instant Pot, and stir through the vegetable soup mix.
3) Pour the vegetable broth on top, and set to Rice for 5 minutes. Then, Quick Release the pressure.
4) Fluff with a fork when done and then serve immediately.

Serving Suggestion: This is the perfect accompaniment to a spicy veggie curry on a cold night.

Tip: Add in frozen veggies too, if you like.

16. Ricotta(GF, LC)

Categories: GF, LC
Serves: 6
Preparation time: 40 minutes
Ingredients:
4 cups whole milk
2 tablespoons white vinegar

Preparation:

1) Pour the milk into the Instant Pot and set to Yoghurt, and Boil.
2) When it beeps (the milk has reached 355F), quick release the pressure.
3) Remove the milk into a pot, and stir in the vinegar. Let the mixture sit for 10 minutes.
4) Line a fine mesh strainer with a muslin, and add the ricotta mix in. Let the liquid drain and then add in a little salt to taste.

Serving Suggestion: Have a super simple but delicious low carb lunch by spreading ricotta onto nut and seed crackers, and topping with fresh basil. It's perfection!

Tip: Once you're perfected this, never buy ricotta from the store again! If you do the math, you'll find out that this version costs less than half than buying it in the store. Pretty good, right?

17. Rosemary Roasted Potatoes(DF, GF, LF, V)

Categories: DF, GF, LF, V
Serves: 6
Preparation time: 35 minutes
Ingredients:
24 oz small red potatoes
2 sprigs fresh rosemary
2 tablespoons olive oil

Preparation:

1) Wash the potatoes and cut them into halves.
2) Pour 1 cup of water into the bottom of the Instant Pot and add in the steaming rack.
3) Cook the potatoes on High Pressure for 5 minutes and then allow natural pressure release for 15 minutes. Then, quick release the rest of the pressure.
4) Remove the potatoes, and pour out the remaining water. Dry the Instant Pot and add in your oil.
5) Set the pot to Saute, and place the potatoes into the oil, cut side down.
6) Add in the rosemary sprigs, breaking them up over the potatoes.
7) Brown the potatoes for 4 minutes on the cut side, and then flip them over to the other side for a further 2 minutes
8) Sprinkle with salt and pepper whilst hot and serve immediately.

Serving Suggestion: I do not have time to reel off the list of dinners that these rosemary potatoes are the perfect accompaniment for! Just know that you'll never go wrong!

Tip: The potatoes will become unstuck from the bottom naturally when they've crisped up. Don't try to remove them before this happens as they will still stick at this point.

18. Sweet Potatoes(DF, GF, LF, V)

Categories: DF, GF, LF, V
Serves: 4
Preparation time: 40 minutes
Ingredients:
4 sweet potatoes

Preparation:
1) Put the steamer basket into your Instant pot and pour in 1 cup of water.
2) Scrub the skins of the sweet potatoes clean, and then add them to the steamer basket.
3) Select the Steam setting for 10 minutes. Then, allow natural release of the pressure for 25 minutes.

Serving Suggestion: Why not change things up a little and have sweet potatoes as a sweet treat? Serve with cinnamon and maple butter, for example.

Tip: If you're using the sweet potatoes for mash or something else where you don't want the skin, then it is super easy to just wash off by running under cold water once they're cooked.

Desserts

1. Apple Crunch(DF)

Categories: DF
Serves: 4
Preparation time: 30 minutes
Ingredients:
3 apples
1 lemon
1 cup dry breadcrumbs
1 teaspoon cinnamon
¼ cup sugar
¼ cup coconut oil

Preparation:

1) Grease a baking dish that will fit into your Instant Pot.
2) Juice and zest the lemon and mix together with the cinnamon, sugar and breadcrumbs.
3) Slice the apples, and then alternate layers of apple and breadcrumb mixture in your baking dish.
4) Pour the coconut oil over the top. Cover the dish tightly with foil.
5) Pour 2 cups of water into the Instant Pot and add in a rack. Place the baking dish onto the rack and cook on High Pressure for 15 minutes and then quick release the pressure.

Serving Suggestion: Ice cream and caramel sauce!

Tip: For an extra crunchy top, place the dish under the grill for a few minutes to crisp up.

2. Banana Bread(DF)

Categories: DF
Serves: 8
Preparation time: 70 minutes
Ingredients:
4 bananas
4 oz coconut oil
2 eggs
2 cups flour
1 teaspoon baking powder

Preparation:

1) Beat the coconut oil and eggs together.
2) Mash the bananas and stir them into the egg mix.
3) Stir in the flour and baking powder, as well as a pinch of salt, until the mixture is well combined.
4) Line a cake tin or loaf tin with parchment paper and pour the batter in.
5) Pour 1 cup of water into the bottom of the Instant Pot and add in the steaming rack. Place the cake tin onto the rack.
6) Cook for 50 minutes on Low Pressure, and allow a 10 minute Natural Release. Quick Release any remaining pressure and pour off any excess moisture before serving.

Serving Suggestion: Warm banana bread is pretty much as close to perfection as you can get on this earth! Spread with a cheeky spreading of all-natural peanut butter or chocolate spread and enjoy!

Tip: Overripe bananas = sweet bananas, which, in a loaf without sugar, is important! If you have some but aren't ready to make a loaf, you can freeze them!

3. Berry Compote(DF, GF, LF, V)

Categories: DF, GF, LF, V
Makes: 1 jar
Preparation time: 25 minutes
Ingredients:
2 cups fresh strawberries
2 tablespoons lemon juice
1 cup fresh blueberries
1 tablespoon corn starch
¾ cup sugar

Preparation:

1) Hull and slice the strawberries and place them into your Instant Pot.
2) Add in half of the blueberries, as well as the lemon juice and the sugar.
3) Cook for 3 minutes on High Pressure, and then naturally release the pressure for 10 minutes.
4) Quick release any remaining pressure.
5) Whisk the cornstarch together with 1 tablespoon of water, and then add it to the compote.
6) Set the Instant Pot to Saute and bring to the boil, stirring constantly.
7) Stir through the remaining blueberries and enjoy!

Serving Suggestion: If all you have laying around is boring old plain vanilla ice cream, then this is a delicious topping choice to make it a little more exciting!

Tip: Use other berries if you prefer!

4. Caramel Flan(GF, LC)

Categories: GF, LC
Serves: 6
Preparation time: 25 minutes
Ingredients:
14 oz sweetened condensed milk
4 eggs
1 cup milk
1 teaspoon vanilla extract
¾ cup sugar

Preparation:

1) In a pan on high heat, add the sugar and stir it to thicken and become a lovely golden caramel. It should take 10-15 minutes.
2) Pour the caramel into an oven-proof dish that'll fit into your Instant Pot and swirl it around to cover the whole base nicely.
3) Beat together the eggs, milk, sweetened condensed milk and the vanilla extract until smooth.
4) Pour the mixture over the top of the caramel, and cover the dish with aluminium foil.
5) Pour 1 ½ cups of water into the bottom of your Instant Pot, and add in the steam rack. Place the dish on top of the rack.
6) Set to High Pressure for 5 minutes, and then allow the pressure to release naturally. Check that the flan is done by inserting a skewer and checking that it comes out clean.

Serving Suggestion: This is the perfect dessert for the middle of the work week, when you're in need of some sugar and have no energy. The great thing is that the likelihood of having all the ingredients to hand at the same time is high!

Tip: If you are a fan of salt and sweet together, add a good amount of salt to your caramel for a yummy salted caramel base.

5. Chocolate Lava Cakes(DF)

Categories: DF
Serves: 4
Preparation time: 15 minutes
Ingredients:
6 tablespoons plain flour
4 eggs
4 oz coconut oil
1 cup dark chocolate chips
1 cup icing sugar

Preparation:

1) Melt the butter and chocolate chips together until smooth.
2) Then, stir in the icing sugar.
3) Add in 3 eggs and just the yolk of the fourth.
4) Grease 4 individual ramekins, and divide the batter evenly between them.
5) Add a rack into the Instant Pot and pour in 1 cup of water.
6) Place the ramekins in and cook on High Pressure for 9 minutes and then quick release the pressure.
7) Turn the ramekins upside down onto plates to serve the lava cakes.

Serving Suggestion: Ice cream and caramel sauce would be a great idea!

Tip: Once you've mastered this, you may want to try a peanut butter lava filling. To do that, mix 4 tablespoons of peanut butter with 1 tablespoon of butter and 2 tablespoons of powdered sugar. Pour the chocolate batter in up to half way, and then spoon in a heaped tablespoon of the peanut mixture, before filling up to the top with the rest of the chocolate batter.

6. Chocolate Puddings(GF, LC)

Categories: GF, LC
Serves: 4
Preparation time: 40 minutes
Ingredients:
6 ½ oz dark chocolate
6 tablespoons sugar
4 eggs
1 ½ cups cream
1 tablespoon vanilla extract

Preparation:

1) Chop the chocolate and stir it together with the sugar.
2) Set the Instant Pot to Saute and add in the cream. Bring it to the boil. Then, stir in the chocolate and sugar mix. Stir until the chocolate is melted and the sugar is dissolved and you're left with a smooth mixture. Let it boil for 2 minutes.
3) Separate the eggs and stir the yolks into the mixture, along with the vanilla extract and a pinch of salt.
4) Then, divide the chocolate mixture evenly between 6 ramekins, and clean out the bottom of the Instant Pot as best you can, but it doesn't have to be perfect at this point.
5) Pour 2 cups of water into the bottom of the Instant Pot, and place the steaming rack inside.
6) Cover the ramekins with foil and place them onto the steaming rack, carefully stacking them onto each other, if needed.
7) Set to High Pressure for 15 minutes and then quick release.

Serving Suggestion: Ice cream baby!

Tip: If dark chocolate isn't your favourite, of course you can substitute it for other kinds of chocolate, or a mix of 2 or 3.

7. GF Key Lime Pie(GF)

Categories: GF
Serves: 6
Preparation time: 40 minutes + 3 hours refrigeration
Ingredients:
14 oz sweetened condensed milk
4 tablespoons melted butter
8 key limes
3 eggs
1 cup gluten-free cookies

Preparation:

1) Pulse the cookies into crumbs and mix with the melted butter. Press the base down into a cake tin that will fit inside your Instant Pot. Place the tin in the freezer until you're made the filling.
2) Juice and zest the limes.
3) Whisk the egg yolks, and then stir the condensed milk into them.
4) Then, add in 2/3 of a cup of lime juice and 1 tablespoon of the zest.
5) Pour the condensed milk mixture over the cookie crumb base.
6) Pour 1 cup of water into your instant pot and add a rack in.
7) Place the key lime pie on the rack and cover with the lid.
8) Cook on High Pressure for 15 minutes, and then allow natural release for 10 minutes.
9) Refrigerate for at least 3 hours before serving.

Serving Suggestion: Use the remaining lime zest and whip it into some cream to serve the pie with.

Tip: It's easier to get the tin out of the Instant Pot if you place a sheet of foil underneath that comes all the way up the sides and out of the top. You can just lift that (with oven gloves on, of course!)

8. Giant Pancake(DF)

Categories: DF
Serves: 4
Preparation time: 50 minutes
Ingredients:
2 ½ teaspoons baking powder
2 eggs
2 cups plain flour
2 tablespoons white sugar
1 ½ cups almond milk

Preparation:

1) Whisk the eggs and milk together.
2) Once smooth, also whisk in the flour, sugar and baking powder.
3) Grease the inside of your Instant Pot thoroughly, concentrating especially on the bottom.
4) Pour in the batter and set the pot on to Low Pressure for 45 minutes.
5) Flip the pancake out, so that the bottom that has become nice and crispy in the cooker is now the top.

Serving Suggestion: Syrup and butter is the way, isn't it? If you like fillings in your pancake, then go ahead and stir in chopped banana, chocolate chips or blueberries.

Tip: If you experience problems with the pot overheating, then set it to rice mode instead.

9. Hibiscus Tea(DF, GF, LF, V)

Categories: DF, GF, LF, V
Serves: 8
Preparation time: 40 minutes
Ingredients:
2 cups dried hibiscus leaves (zobo)
1 cup sugar
1 cup pineapple chunks
1 teaspoon fresh ginger

Preparation:

1) Thoroughly rinse the hibiscus leaves.
2) Pour 10 cups of water into the Instant Pot, on Saute mode and mince in the ginger.
3) Add in the sugar and stir until it's dissolved.
4) Stir in the hibiscus leaves and the pineapple.
5) Cook on High Pressure for 10 minutes, and then release the pressure naturally.
6) Strain the mixture and discard the hibiscus leaves. Use the pineapple to garnish the glasses if you want, or discard it too.

Serving Suggestion: This drink just screams summer! Serve in cute Mason jars with ice and a slice (of lemon!) and an adorable striped straw.

Tip: This drink is not so common in some parts of the world, so if you're wanting to 'try before you buy', look out for a drink called 'Jamaica' in Mexican or other Latino/ Central American style restaurants or shops. Or, take a trip to Mexico, for research purposes of course!

10. Honey & Pine Nut Mousse(DF)

Categories: DF
Serves: 6
Preparation time: 45 minutes
Ingredients:
2 eggs
1 ¼ cups pine nuts
1 ¼ cups coconut cream
1 cup honey

Preparation:

1) Choose an oven proof casserole dish that will fit into your Instant Pot and line it with parchment paper.
2) Mix the eggs, honey, coconut cream and half of the pine nuts until smooth in a blender.
3) Stir the rest of the whole pine nuts through the mousse and pour it evenly into your dish.
4) Pour 1 cup of water into the bottom of the Instant Pot, and place a rack inside. Place your dish on top of the rack.
5) Cook on Low Pressure for 25 minutes, and then allow the pressure to naturally release.
6) Allow the mousse to cool fully and then invert it out of the dish and onto a plate.
7) Refrigerate overnight and enjoy!

Serving Suggestion: Serve with a mountain of fresh fruit for a sweet and light dessert.

Tip: Allow the mousse to cool totally before trying to turn it out, to reduce the risk of breaking to as little as possible.

11. Japanese White Chocolate Cheesecake(GF, LC)

Categories: GF, LC
Serves: 6
Preparation time: 40 minutes
Ingredients:
4 oz cream cheese
4 oz white chocolate
2 eggs
Icing sugar for dusting

Preparation:

1) Choose a cake pan that will fit inside your Instant Pot and line with parchment paper.
2) Separate the eggs and refrigerate the whites.
3) Melt the white chocolate and whisk it together with the cream cheese until smooth.
4) Then, whisk in the egg yolks.
5) Beat the egg whites into very stiff, glossy peaks and then fold them into the mixture, 1 third at a time. Pour the batter into the prepared cake tin.
6) Add 1 ½ cups of water to the bottom of your Instant Pot and place the steam rack inside.
7) Place the pan on the rack, ensuring that it doesn't touch the water.
8) Set the pot to High Pressure for 17 minutes and then naturally release the pressure.
9) Refrigerate for a few hours and dust with icing sugar before serving.

Serving Suggestion: Serve with some ice cream or sorbet of some Japanese flavour, like lychee or saki!

Tip: I cannot stress enough the importance of really having stiff peaks when you beat the whites. The tips should be standing straight up. If they're not that stiff, your cake will collapse!

12. Lemon Curd(GF)

Categories: GF
Makes: 3 small jars
Preparation time: 30 minutes
Ingredients:
6 tablespoons butter
4 eggs
2 teaspoons lemon zest
1 cup sugar
2/3 cup lemon juice

Preparation:

1) Cream together the butter and sugar until smooth.
2) Add in 2 whole eggs and then incorporate just the yolks of the other.
3) Add in the lemon juice (don't worry if it looks curdled, it will fix whilst cooking).
4) Divide the mixture into the 2 jars and tightly seal the tops.
5) Pour 1 ½ cups of water into the bottom of the Instant Pot and place in a steaming rack.
6) Put the jars onto the rack and cook on High Pressure for 10 minutes. Then, Naturally Release the pressure for 10 minutes, before quick releasing the rest.
7) Stir in the zest, and put the lids back on the jars, until just caught.
8) Refrigerate overnight.

Serving Suggestion: Spread thickly on a big hunk of bread is the best way to enjoy this!

Tip: Switch the lemons out for oranges or limes for a different kind of citrus curd!

13. Mini Pumpkin Bakes(DF, GF)

Categories: DF, GF
Serves: 8
Preparation time: 45 minutes
Ingredients:
48 oz pumpkin
2 eggs
1 cup coconut milk
1 teaspoon pumpkin pie spice
¾ cup maple syrup

Preparation:

1) De-seed the pumpkin and chop it up into cubes.
2) Pour 1 cup of water into the Instant Pot and then add a steaming basket in. Put the pumpkin cubes on the steaming rack. Cook for 9 minutes at High Pressure.
3) Meanwhile, beat together the eggs, maple syrup, coconut milk, pumpkin pie spice and a pinch of salt.
4) When the time is up, Quick Release the pressure and, when the pumpkin is cool enough, peel the skin off.
5) Strain the pumpkin and then mash the flesh into a pulp.
6) Blend the pumpkin with the eggs mixture.
7) Fill up the water in the Instant Pot to 1 cup again, if necessary, and keep the steam rack in there.
8) Divide the pumpkin mixture between 8 ramekins and cook for 10 minutes at High Pressure.
9) Allow the pressure to naturally release for 10 minutes, and then Quick Release the rest.

Serving Suggestion: Whip up some coconut cream and sprinkle some chopped pecans on the top for a little taste of the Fall!

Tip: You could set aside the strained water from the pumpkin and use it in other recipes, in place of butter or margarine.

14. Orange Creme Brulee(GF, LC)

Categories: GF, LC
Serves: 6
Preparation time: 30 minutes
Ingredients:
9 tablespoons sugar
6 eggs
2 cups heavy cream
1 teaspoon vanilla extract
1 teaspoon orange extract

Preparation:

1) Set the Instant Pot to Saute, and begin heating the cream on a low heat until it's simmering.
2) Separate the eggs and mix the yolks together with 5 tablespoons of sugar.
3) Slowly add the heated cream into the egg yolk mix, whisking with a fork all the time.
4) Then, add in the vanilla and orange extracts.
5) Divide the mixture between your 6 ramekins and cover each one with foil.
6) Place a rack into your Instant Pot, and add water in up until 1 inch below the rack.
7) Place the ramekins on the rack, stacking them on top of each other if you need to.
8) Set to High Pressure and cook for 9 minutes, and then quick release.
9) Remove the foil to let the crème brulees cool, and then, when you're ready to serve, sprinkle the tops with sugar and caramelise with a torch or under the grill.

Serving Suggestion: Dessert wine, maybe?

Tip: We've gone for orange extract, but if you prefer, you can use another kind of extract for a different flavour.

15. Oreo Cake(DF, V)

Categories: DF, V
Serves: 6
Preparation time: 30 minutes
Ingredients:
20 Oreos
4 tablespoons sugar
1 teaspoon baking soda
1 teaspoon baking powder
½ cup almond milk

Preparation:

1) Line a cake tin that will fit into your Instant Pot with parchment paper.
2) Add ½ a cup of salt into the bottom of the pot.
3) Pulse the Oreos down into a fine powder. Stir the powder together with the baking powder, baking soda, sugar and milk. Mix well and then pour the batter into the cake tin.
4) Cook on Low Pressure for 20-25 minutes and then Quick Release the pressure.

Serving Suggestion: Add whatever you want on top! A great choice though, is caramel sauce and chocolate chips!

Tip: This cake doesn't have a lot of moisture in it, so err on the side of less cooking time rather than more.

16. Raspberry & Vanilla Rice Pudding(DF, GF, LF, V)

Categories: DF, GF, LF, V
Serves: 6-8
Preparation time: 25 minutes
Ingredients:
3 tablespoons smooth raspberry jam
2 cups vanilla almond milk
1 cup rice
1 teaspoon vanilla extract
¼ cup brown sugar

Preparation:

1) Set the Instant Pot to Sauté and add 1 cup of water, the milk, sugar and raspberry jam.
2) Cook down and stir until the jam and sugar are dissolved and melted.
3) Then, stir in the rice and vanilla extract.
4) Select the Porridge setting and allow it to release the pressure naturally.

Serving Suggestion: Top with extra fresh raspberries and sprinkle with cinnamon.

Tip: Easily make this recipe dairy-free by using plant-based milk.

17. Steamed Apples(DF, GF, LF, V)

Categories: DF, GF, LF, V
Serves: 6
Preparation time: 40 minutes
Ingredients:
6 apples
1 cup red wine
1 teaspoon cinnamon
½ cup raisins
½ cup brown sugar

Preparation:

1) Core the apples and then place them in the Instant Pot.
2) Sprinkle in the raisins, cinnamon and sugar, and pour in the wine.
3) Cook for 10 minutes on High Pressure, and allow natural release.
4) Serve one apple with a generous scoop of cooking liquid and enjoy!

Serving Suggestion: This is a sophisticated dessert that won't wreak havoc with your waistline! If you're in need of a mid-week sweet treat, you won't need to feel bad about this one.

Tip: Use cider in place of wine, if you prefer.

18. Tapioca Pudding(DF, GF, LF, V)

Categories: DF, GF, LF, V
Serves: 2
Preparation time: 15 minutes
Ingredients:
3 tablespoons instant tapioca
2 ¾ cups soya milk
1 egg
1 teaspoon vanilla extract
1/3 cup sugar

Preparation:
1) Mix together the vanilla extract, sugar and tapioca.
2) Whisk the egg and soya milk together and then stir the mixture into the tapioca mixture until everything is well combined.
3) Spray the inside of your Instant Pot with non-stick cooking spray and pour the mixture in.
4) Steam on High Pressure for 7 minutes and then allow the pressure to do a natural release.
5) Stir well and serve, with whatever toppings you desire!

Serving Suggestion: I would pile this up with berries!

Tip: If your tapioca doesn't look thick enough, set the pot to Saute and let the mixture bubble away for another few minutes until it's reached your desired consistency.

19. Yoghurt(GF, LC)

Categories: GF, LC
Serves: 6
Preparation time: At least 8 ½ hours
Ingredients:
64 fl oz whole milk
3 tablespoons plain yoghurt

Preparation:

1) Pour the milk into your Instant Pot and then select the Yoghurt and Boil settings.
2) When the boiling is done, and you hear the beep, let it sit for another 5 minutes.
3) Remove the pot of milk and set on a rack. Put in a thermometer and stir occasionally until the temperature has reduced down to 115F.
4) Add the yoghurt into a bowl with 2/3 of a cup of the milk.
5) Place everything back into the Instant Pot and press the Yoghurt setting.
6) Leave it on Yoghurt setting to curdle for 8 hours, and then enjoy your homemade yoghurt!

Serving Suggestion: Well, now you can use this is a base for your breakfast or snack, and top and flavour with whatever you like!

Tip: To cool down the milk quicker, place the bowl in an ice bath and whisk.

The Final Words

Thanks again for your reading about this Instant Pot recipe book! With these all 101 mouth-watering and delicious recipes, hope you have had your favorite ones! Eat easy, eat healthy, then be longevity! Best wishes to all dear readers!

66852304R00068

Made in the USA
Middletown, DE
15 March 2018